HEGEL'S ABSOLUTE

SUNY series in Hegelian Studies
William Desmond, editor

HEGEL'S ABSOLUTE

An Introduction to Reading the *Phenomenology of Spirit*

Donald Phillip Verene

State University of New York Press

Published by
State University of New York Press, Albany

Printed in the United States of America

For information, address State University of New York Press,
194 Washington Avenue, Suite 305, Albany, NY 12210-2384

Production by Diane Ganeles
Marketing by Anne M. Valentine

Library of Congress Cataloging-in-Publication Data

Verene, Donald Phillip, 1937–
Hegel's absolute : an introduction to reading The phenomenology of spirit / Donald Phillip Verene.
p. cm. — (SUNY series in Hegelian studies)
Includes bibliographical references (p.) and index.
ISBN-13: 978-0-7914-6963-7 (hardcover : alk. paper)
ISBN-13: 978-0-7914-6964-4 (pbk. : alk. paper)
1. Hegel, Georg Wilhelm Friedrich, 1770–1831. Phänomenologie des Geistes. 2. Spirit. 3. Consciousness. 4. Truth. 5. Phenomenology. I. Title. II. Series.

B2929.V46 2007
193—dc22

2006003850

10 9 8 7 6 5 4 3 2 1

A quite special, though purely negative science, general phenomenology (*phaenomenologia generalis*), seems to be presupposed by metaphysics.

—Kant to Lambert, September 2, 1770

Hegel had the stuff of one of the greatest humorists among philosophers; Socrates is the only other one who had a similar method.

—Bertolt Brecht, *Flüchtlingsgespräche*, 1941

Contents

Preface

Hegel's texts make unusual demands on the reader. This is especially true of the *Phenomenology of Spirit*, commonly regarded as the most difficult text in the history of philosophy. What Hegel intends cannot be presented as a summary of the results of his investigations. The course of spirit's development in all its forms is re-created as a whole in Hegel's exposition, and this full path must be traveled by the reader. Hegel says: "The *length* of this path has to be endured, because, for one thing, each moment is necessary; and further, each moment has to be *lingered* over, because each is itself a complete individual shape, and one is only viewed in absolute perspective when its determinateness is regarded as a concrete whole, or the whole is regarded as uniquely qualified by that determination" (par. 29).

Spirit "has had the patience to pass through these shapes over the long passage of time, and to take upon itself the enormous labour of world-history" (ibid.). Hegel has had the patience to bring these shapes together in his book and the reader must have the patience to comprehend them page by page. It is not sufficient for the reader to study the text from an external point of view. One must make its science for oneself. Hegel says: "What, therefore, is important in the *study* of *science*, is that one should take on oneself the strenuous effort of the notion [*Begriff*]" (par. 58). The reader must strive not simply to pass from one shape of spirit to the next but to aim to know each one, to think through each one, in the manner of the *Begriff* and grasp the process as a whole. This requires the reader to acquire the mentality of speculative philosophy.

The greatest stumbling block to comprehending Hegel's work and studying his science is propensity to argumentation (*raisonnement*). Hegel says: "Such reasoning adopts a negative attitude towards the content it apprehends; it knows how to refute it and destroy it. That something is *not* the case, is a merely negative insight, a dead end which does not lead to a new content beyond itself" (par. 59). Argumentation has the further problem of the passivity of the subject. The passive subject or self that is at the center of argumentation has no essential connection to the object of thought and can offer no advance in knowing. In speculative thinking the subject is actively engaged in altering itself in relation to the object. What it thinks alters what it is. Philosophical texts that portray this self-altering process of knowing, rather than just offering arguments or reflections of common sense, try the reader's ability to the limit.

Hegel says: "This abnormal inhibition of thought is in large measure the source of the complaints regarding the unintelligibility of philosophical writings from individuals who otherwise possess the educational requirements for understanding them. Here we see the reason behind one particular complaint so often made against them: that so much has to be read over and over before it can be understood—a complaint whose burden is presumed to be quite outrageous, and, if justified, to admit of no defence" (par. 63). The reading of a philosophical work is never in principle a single act. Philosophical reading is a repetitive act. Hegel says, further: "We learn by experience that we meant something other than we meant to mean; and this correction of our meaning compels our knowing to go back to the proposition, and understand it in some other way" (ibid.).

What might be added to Hegel's advice of a practical nature for the reader who is to begin the reading of the *Phenomenology*? I have three suggestions: the first derives from principles of rhetoric, the second from Hegel's conception of language, and the third from what I believe to be the general nature of philosophical texts.

1. Each section of the work should be read three times: first to grasp the meaning of the section as a whole, second to grasp the transitions from point to point within its thought, and third to grasp the particular phrases or modes of expression used to make its central ideas comprehensible and memorable.

These three readings correspond to the three classical principles of composition in rhetoric as found in the Roman textbook on rhetoric of Quintilian: *inventio*, the discovery of materials; *dispositio*, their arrangement; *elocutio*, their formulation in language (III.3). Any work is composed in this way, whether or not its author is conscious of these principles. They are natural aspects of composition. No work can be complete that does not have these elements. Thus any work can be read so as to grasp each of them as a level within it. A reader approaching a work in this manner will come away from it with a good comprehension of its contents. This does not mean, as Hegel points out, that one does not need to go back many times to an important philosophical work. Philosophical works are like songs; their meaning is revealed in repetition. They must be heard over and over again.

2. Hegel's language has been thought to be dense, obscure, and full of special terms. Hegel wrote to Johann Heinrich Voss (May 1805) that Voss had made Homer speak German, Martin Luther had made the Bible, and now he, Hegel, intended to make philosophy speak German. Immanuel Kant writes a Latinized German. Hegel intends to write in German the way Dante chose to write in Florentine Italian instead of Latin. None of Hegel's famous terms—*Geist, aufheben, Begriff*—is a technical term. They all are words of ordinary German. Some of them happen to be terms deeply grounded in the *Weltanschauung* of the German language and cannot be easily rendered into English.

There is a decision every philosophy must make: whether to ground its basic concepts in terms of its own invention or to extract its meanings from common speech. The father of those philosophers who chose the latter is Socrates, who speaks the language of the *agora* and who is accused of using the language of tradesmen and craftsmen. Hegel's approach to philosophical speech is Socratic. Like Socrates, he takes words of ordinary language and begins to press their meanings toward further meanings by developing them into new contexts, all the while using the words any German speaker knows. How Hegel accomplishes this transformation of meanings can be seen by consulting the remarks on Hegel's terms in the appendix. Hegel always speaks in the *agora*, although what he is speaking about, as he says, will cause common sense to walk on its head.

3. Hegel, like most great philosophers, says everything three ways. First he will make a point in purely intellectual or discursive terms, perhaps using terms such as "in-itself" and "for-itself," or assertions such as "Substance becomes Subject." Second, he will often use a common-sense example or analogy, such as saying that zoology is not the same as "all animals." Third, he will use metaphor and irony, such as "the night in which all cows are black," the "Bacchanalian revel," or the "Golgotha of the Spirit." His modes of expression will pass back and forth among discursive, commonsensical, and tropic.

In his *Autobiography* R. G. Collingwood says that philosophy is essentially questions and answers. Hans-Georg Gadamer in *Truth and Method* is one of the few who have noticed the importance of Collingwood's observation. Collingwood was a Hegelian thinker, and the emphasis on a dialectic of questions and answers over and against argumentation fits well with Hegel's view of argumentation as an obstacle to achieving speculative thinking. A question always requires a starting point. The *archai* in Hegel's text are always expressed in images: the image of the master-servant, the inverted world, the unhappy consciousness, the beautiful soul, and so forth. Any philosophical text depends upon images; they are always present. The reader can look first not for arguments in the work but for these root images. Once found, the reader can look for the questions that can be drawn forth from the images. The reader will then see how the image is directing and providing support for the question, which carries the reasoning process of the text forward. What are the images? What are the questions embedded in them?

The aim of this introduction is not to make a series of summaries of all the parts of the *Phenomenology* but to offer the reader a way to approach parts A and B of Hegel's work—his doctrine of consciousness and self-consciousness. My thesis is that once the dialectic of these two primary parts of Hegel's work is grasped, nothing of what Hegel says, at least in principle, is closed to the reader. In his preface, introduction, and parts A and B of the work, Hegel brings forth the essentials of his whole form of thought.

This method of approaching Hegel's work is supplemented in chapters 9 and 10, by an overview of Hegel's stages of reason and spirit, and by a view of the dialectic between religion and absolute knowing that occurs at the end of the *Phenomenology*. The reader may find these last two chapters useful, as they offer a place to stand when taking on the often complicated details of the second "half" of the work. They offer a way to keep the forest in sight while confronting the trees of each of Hegel's stages.

My remarks on the various features of the *Phenomenology* constitute a point of view that I believe brings out the originality of Hegel. My aim is not Hegel "made simple." The reader may not agree with all that is said, nor, in the interest of the pursuit of philosophy, do I think that the reader should agree, but it is a place to stand from which the inner form of Hegel's thought may be seen. I have not attempted to conceal my own eccentricities in regard to how I see Hegel's originality. What follows differs from what is to be found in encyclopedia articles, standard commentaries, and textbook chapters on Hegel. This work is directed to the advanced or intermediate reader of philosophy who has some understanding of Kant, and to the professional philosopher who has interest in the revival of speculative philosophy. I also believe that much of what is said in these chapters may be useful to any reader who has decided to attempt the colossus of Hegel. To my mind, the greatest interpreter of Hegel in our time was John Findlay. In conversation and in his writings, he, more than anyone else, captured not only the sense but the spirit of Hegel. The reader would benefit from any of his works.

These chapters extend and restate some of the views of my *Hegel's Recollection* (1985), but what I say is specifically directed to the problem of reading the *Phenomenology*. Readers who wish fuller discussions of such issues as Hegel's doubling of the in-itself, the logic of the inverted world, or the importance of Hegel's criticism of phrenology, may wish to consult the earlier work. The chapters that follow exhibit my conviction that the two central principles of Hegel's philosophy are recollection (*Erinnerung*) and speculation. Hegel identifies them with reason (*Vernunft*). To comprehend these two principles is to comprehend the Hegelian point of view.

Quotations from Hegel's *Phenomenology of Spirit* are from A. V. Miller's translation, occasionally modified by my translation, and cited by Miller's paragraph enumeration. Miller's translation is at present the most-read English edition of the *Phenomenology*. The earlier translation by J. B. Baillie is often less accurate to the original, but Baillie's renderings of Hegel's metaphors and key phrases generally achieve a higher English and they are more memorable than Miller's. The reader of the *Phenomenology* in English may wish to consult both. Full bibliographic references for these translations and for all other works that appear in the text are in the list of works cited.

The first draft of this work was written in May 1996, on the terrace of the villa of my long-time friend Marco Olivetti, at Lavinio, the ancient Lavinium, on the Italian coast near Rome, where Aeneas is said to have landed. I thank Professor Olivetti of the philosophy faculty of the University of Rome "La Sapienza" for his generosity as host, and the University of Rome for the generosity of my appointment as research fellow while I was writing this work. The connection with Aeneas is apt, for Hegel's work is a journey in which spirit enters its own underworld, its own "highway of despair." As the reader travels from one illusory stage of consciousness to another, inspecting the shades of spirit, the reader realizes that the journey is one of self-knowledge. The golden bough that Hegel offers the reader to exit this underworld is the absolute that will emerge at the end of the journey with the realization that the reader has possessed it all along; hence the title of this book.

I am grateful to the several "generations" of graduate and advanced undergraduate students on whom I have tried out these ideas of how to read Hegel. I have benefited much from their responses to versions of these chapters. As always, I am grateful to Molly Black Verene for transcribing these chapters from my handwriting and putting the manuscript in good order. I thank my colleagues who have generously read and offered comments on this work: Thora Ilin Bayer, Ann Hartle, Donald Livingston, David Lovekin, and William Willeford. Philosophy depends on friendship.

It is a pleasure to have this work appear on the 200th anniversary of the publication of the *Phenomenology of Spirit* (1807).

CHAPTER 1

Hegel's Preface: Reflection versus Speculation

Hegel wrote his preface to the *Phenomenology* after the work was finished. It is a general statement of his system, not simply an opening to the *Phenomenology*. The preface is a whole, a statement of the nature of true philosophy that compresses in one narrative more themes than a single set of remarks can cover. The preface is Hegel's phenomenology of philosophy; it treats the various forms of philosophizing and delineates their defects. In a sense the preface is the completion of the section on absolute knowing. The book is itself a circle, the form Hegel attributes to the system as a whole. A theme that runs through the center of the preface is Hegel's criticism of reflection and the understanding (*Verstand*) as capable of producing true philosophy and his characterization of speculation and reason (*Vernunft*) as the replacement for this inadequate form of philosophizing.

We find two sets of images in the preface. On the first page Hegel speaks of anatomy as being not a true science but only an "aggregate of information" (par. 1). Because it is a knowledge of only the parts of the body regarded as inanimate, we lack, in anatomy, a knowledge of the living body itself, of its principle of life. On the second page Hegel introduces the contrasting image of the bud of a plant producing a blossom that becomes a fruit. He characterizes this as an image of "organic unity" (par. 2) and as representing stages of necessity in the life of the whole. He plays on the image of the dead, the corpse (par. 3), and on the concrete richness of life (par. 4).

Further, he compares spirit with the birth of a child and to bringing forth a "new world" (pars. 11–13). Later, in sharp contrast to this, he speaks of *triadic form* reducing all to a "lifeless schema" (*lebloses Schema*) (par. 50). He speaks of "a synoptic table like a skeleton with tickets stuck all over it," the flesh and blood having been stripped off. Such schematic orderings, he says, are the "products of reflection," and he says "all are equally products of the lifeless understanding and external cognition" (par. 51). He speaks of spirit being deprived of life, "of being flayed and then seeing its skin wrapped around a lifeless knowledge and its conceit" (par. 52). In contrast to this is his famous image that "The true is thus the Bacchanalian revel at which not a member is sober; yet because each member collapses as soon as he drops out, the revel is just as much a scene of transparent unbroken calm" (par. 47). There is no schematic order to the revel; it is an activity of a whole, alive within its own limits. Hegel says that the understanding schematizes experience, "a table of contents is all that it offers" (par. 53).

The understanding, which proceeds through reflection on the object, produces, in thought, a world that is dead. All objects are fully categorized and rendered lifeless, labeled, like parts of a skeleton, or pigeon-holed, like boxes in a grocer's stall. Reason, which proceeds speculatively, seeks out the principle of motion or life that is within the object, that makes the object, so to speak, what it is. Reflective understanding grasps the body as an anatomically ordered *substance*. Speculative reason goes within the body to its spirit to grasp its principle as a living *subject*. The images Hegel is using fix for us the *archai* of the question he is asking. What is this question?

The answer to this lies principally with Kant, with transcendental philosophy and critique. In his effort to answer David Hume and to secure, for the understanding, its own categories of experience, not derived from the senses, Kant forces himself to abandon reason. This causes Kant to formulate a very limited notion of experience, in which reason plays no role in the constitution of the object. Once one enters the world of critique there is no way out, no way to restore reason to its rightful place. Reason is sacrificed to reflection and to the trap of the transcendental. Even as Kant tries to loosen the bonds of critique, in the *Third Critique*, and include aesthetic and organic natural form within his system, he finds he cannot make the ideas that govern reason constitutive of the being of the object.

The *Third Critique* may show us Kant at his most attractive moment, but he still finds himself and his "fellow worker" bound to the Caucasus of critique. Kant finds he cannot escape from the island, that in the *First Critique* he says is the pure understanding, "enclosed by nature itself within unalterable limits. It is a land of truth—enchanting name!—surrounded by a wide and stormy ocean, the native home of illusion, where many a fog bank and many a swiftly melting iceberg give the deceptive appearance of farther shores, deluding the adventurous seafarer ever anew with empty hopes, and engaging him in enterprises which he never can abandon and yet is unable to carry to completion" (A235–36; B294–95). Kant's warning about reason echoes René Descartes' warning in the *Discourse on Method* to those who would listen to fictitious narratives. They are liable, Descartes says, "to fall into the excesses of the knights-errant in our tales of chivalry, and to conceive plans beyond their powers" (pt. 1). To seek the realm of reason is to seek the *Abenteuer* of deluded seafarers or the *extravagance* of paladins tilting at windmills in philosophy, engaging in fictions as if they were real life.

Hegel singles out Kant's schematism as the great flaw of the understanding because it is often taken as the great achievement of transcendental reflection. The schematism is often taken to be the element in the *First Critique* that leads to the sympathetic treatment of organic form in the *Third*. The schema is the leading example of the *triadic form* that is at the foundation of Kant's philosophy of critique. The problem stated in Kant's famous assertion, "Thoughts without concepts are empty, intuitions without concepts are blind" (A51; B75), is thought to be solved by the schema, that through which intuitions and concepts are held together. The schema is claimed to be the concrete form from which they are factored out. Hegel says: "Kant rediscovered this triadic form by instinct, but in his work it was still lifeless and uncomprehended" (par. 50).

Hegel says the formalism inherent in this manner of thinking "imagines that it has comprehended and expressed the nature and life of a form when it has endowed it with some determination of the schema as a predicate" (ibid.). In other words, coming upon a problem, this way of thinking just makes a further distinction, then considers the problem overcome. How is the concept related to the intuition? They are part of a third thing, the schema, and like this on down the line. Hegel says: "Such predicates can be multiplied to infinity, since in this way each determination or form can again be used as a form or moment in the case of an other, and each can gratefully perform the same service for an other. In this sort of circle of reciprocity one never learns what the thing itself is, nor what the one or the other is" (ibid.).

What is Hegel's question, exactly? Given the important success of critique, of rescuing philosophy from both rationalism and empiricism, is there any way now to rescue reason from critique and reestablish it in some sense similar to the ancients' principle of *nous* and to recover a doctrine of ideas that makes them more than sirens calling out to the philosophical seafarer from the fog banks of illusion? Hegel, finishing the *Phenomenology* in 1807, having worked out the full nature of his system several years earlier, in Jena, could see what we often have difficulty in seeing—that Kant's philosophy is the pinnacle of Enlightenment thought. In his doctrine of critique Kant has taken *raisonnement*, that power natural to reflection, and made its distinction-making power the systematic activity of the understanding. The understanding is the creation of Descartes' *Discourse* and John Locke's *Essay*, which develop it in terms of the idea of reflection as the central activity of the mind in its act of knowing.

In the *Science of Logic*, Hegel says that ancient metaphysics believed thought could achieve a true knowledge of things, "But *reflective* understanding took possession of philosophy [Aber der *reflektierende* Verstand bemächtigte sich der Philosophie]." He says the view that philosophy is essentially reflective has become a slogan (*Schlagwort*) (p. 45). Through reflection formulated as critique we only know the object as a phenomenon, "as reflected," and by transcendentally turning reflection on the knower we know the necessary conditions under which the phenomenal object can be known. For we moderns, this is our secure island. The ancients, and Hegel, thought they could know more.

How does Hegel move from the established fact of reflection to speculation? To do this he first embraces a doctrine of the absolute. A doctrine of the absolute means that "The true is the whole [*Das Wahre ist das Ganze*]" (par. 20). Critique moves across experience, not within its inner life. Since critique is a doctrine of the part, analyzing this kind of knowledge and then that, we never can produce the whole. To analyze a great number of words will not produce a language and to analyze a great number of phenomena will not produce a world. "The true *as* the whole" is what we must begin with, and it is a circle. Speculative truth is always a circle. The true, Hegel says, "is the process of its own becoming, the circle that presupposes its end as its goal, having its end also as its beginning" (par. 18).

We cannot achieve the absolute by a formalism of the idea any more than we can achieve it by a formalism of the schema. To relate the contents of experience to the idea externally, showing how each instance is an instance of the absolute is what Hegel calls a "monochromatic formalism" (par. 15). It is a form of thought that repeats the same formula in the same way in relation to whatever it encounters. This way of thinking notices the connections among things and then passes on to the assertion that in the absolute all is one. This is an absolute in which A = A, or the "night in which all cows are black" (par. 16). It is a static form of speculation because there is no principle of self-development whereby the particular determinations of things are comprehended as transforming themselves into larger and larger wholes so that the whole itself is articulated in terms of the particular determinations it encompasses.

Hegel attributes this formalistic or empty absolute of pure identity to Friedrich Schelling. He regards Schelling as having moved from the subjective idealism of Kant to the objective idealism of the absolute, but as not having overcome the formalism inherent in reflection by so doing. The other sense of the absolute Hegel rejects is one he attributes to Friedrich Jacobi, Novalis, and Friedrich von Schlegel. They attempt to replace reflection with *edification* and *enthusiasm* (par. 7). On this view the absolute is to be reached directly by insight and intuition. It is to be not thought but felt. Hegel says: "For the absolute is not supposed to be comprehended, it is to be felt and intuited; not the *Begriff* of the absolute, but the feeling and intuition of it, must govern what is said, and must be expressed by it" (par. 6). The absolute as an object of edification is connected to the "beautiful," the "holy," the "eternal," "religion," and "love" (par. 7). Hegel says these are held out to entice us to embrace such a position.

Transcendental reflection (see Kant's *First Critique*, A262; B317 and A260; B316) cannot be opposed by a formalism of the absolute nor by its intuition through edification. It can only be opposed by what Kant has excluded as constitutive of the object—reason (*Vernunft*). What is the relationship of reason to reflection? Hegel says "the activity of dissolution is the power and work of the *understanding*, the most astonishing and mightiest of powers, or rather the absolute power" (par. 32). Reason does not dissolve experience into its elements. Hegel says: "Reason is *purposive activity*" (par. 22). The understanding's uses of reflection, which are directed solely to the object with the subject simply attached as the "I think," is the opposite of reason. Properly used, reflection is part of the true and part of reason. Hegel says: "Reason is, therefore, misunderstood when reflection is excluded from the true, and is not grasped as a positive moment of the absolute. It is reflection that makes the true a result, but it is equally reflection that overcomes the antithesis between the process of its becoming and the result, for this becoming is also simple, and therefore not different from the form of the true which shows itself as *simple* in its result; the process of becoming is rather just this return into simplicity" (par. 21).

Reflection placed at the service of reason is the basis of speculation. Hegel must take up reflection and absorb it into speculation, thus passing beyond it. The fundamental point on which the *Phenomenology* turns is Hegel's claim that *substance* becomes *subject*. He says: "everything turns on grasping and expressing the true, not only as *substance*, but equally as *subject*" (par. 17). Kantian formalism cannot get beyond substance; it can offer the object of reflection only as externally ordered. Such reflection cannot offer us the *inner form* of the object. The object becomes something only when it is externalized from what it is in itself and is taken up by the knower as the phenomenal object. The phenomenal object is functional, but the thing-in-itself is substantive.

Speculation requires us to approach the object as not substance but subject, as having an inner life—not simply, so to speak, as a body with anatomy but as a living body governed by spirit. Applicable here is A. N. Whitehead's concept in *Process and Reality* of "vacuous actuality" (pp. 43; 253). Understood as substance, the object is vacuous in its actuality, a mere phenomenon for the knower to schematize in the production of judgments. Approached as subject, the object, like reason, is internally ordered, its actuality is not vacuous, not inert. It has an "inside." Reflection at the service of reason becomes an activity of mediation. To know something under the aspect of the true is to know it as subject, as Hegel says: "Something that is reflected into itself, a subject" (par. 23). He says: "Only this self-*restoring* sameness, or this reflection in otherness within itself—not an *original* or *immediate* unity as such—is the true" (par. 18). He says that spirit as substance "is nothing but its own acquisition of self-consciousness, the bringing-about of its own becoming and reflection into itself" (par. 28).

Reflection in the service of reason becomes a process of consciousness wherein the knower meets itself in the known. Reflection becomes an activity internal to what is known rather than an external formation of it. Reflection is taken up into dialectic, which is the science of spirit or the organic unity of the whole. Spirit is "reflection which is itself simple, and which is for itself immediacy as such, *being* that is reflected into itself" (par. 26). Dialectic is reflection turning back on itself, which can capture in thought the self-movement that is substance become subject.

Dialectic enters into the content of the thing, which is in contrast to the formal understanding, which, Hegel says: "Instead of entering into the immanent content of the thing, it is forever surveying the whole and standing above the particular existence of which it is speaking, i.e. it does not see it at all" (par. 53). Argumentation or *raisonnement*, that the understanding can practice, "is reflection into the empty 'I,' the vanity of its own knowing" (par. 59). Mathematical cognition is also inadequate as a model for a science of spirit, for mathematical truths are true independently from whatever proof we may subjectively use to establish them. Their proofs do not form a necessary part of their result. Propositions that state ordinary facts or that state historical conclusions should be affirmed or denied straightway, depending on the evidence.

Thinking that apprehends the true as the whole and can thus produce a science of spirit requires a different sense of the proposition than that which attaches a subject to a predicate to state a particular truth. This requires what Hegel calls the "speculative proposition" or "speculative sentence"—*spekulativer Satz* (par. 61). The speculative sentence or what he also calls the "philosophical proposition" (ibid.) is Hegel's special idea in the preface. It has within it the dialectical motion necessary to present consciousness as alive and self-developing through its determinate shapes to the organic whole of spirit as "absolute knowing."

With it we can distinguish Hegel's phenomenology, which is based in a speculative use of reason from the phenomenology of Edmund Husserl, which remains a reflective phenomenology. Husserl says: "The phenomenological method operates exclusively in acts of reflection" (*Ideas*, sec. 77). Husserl's phenomenology is a descriptive, schematic phenomenology of the contents of experience. We may also distinguish Hegel's speculative reason from Gadamer's "hermeneutic reflection." Gadamer in *Truth and Method* says: "What role does reason play in the context of human practice? In every case it takes the general form of reflection" (p. 569). Indeed, the legacy of Descartes, Locke, G. W. Leibniz, and Kant is the unexamined tenet of modern philosophy that to think philosophically is to reflect.

Regarded from the standpoint of speculative reason, reflection immediately lacks two things: a principle of "inversion" and a principle of "determinate negation." Hegel says: "The immediate existence of spirit, *consciousness*, contains the two moments of knowing and the objectivity negative to knowing" (par. 36). Speculation or dialectical reason follows consciousness as it turns its object to its opposite, as it inverts the truth it holds to in one moment to the opposite that it holds to in the next. Hegel says: "Let science be in its own self what it may, relatively to immediate self-consciousness it presents itself in an inverted posture" (par. 26). Science, Hegel says, causes natural consciousness to walk on its head (ibid.). He says "the science of this pathway is the science of the *experience* which consciousness goes through" (par. 36). The movement of consciousness from one moment to the other is not the simple negation of argumentation (*raisonnement*) when it refutes something as false. In the actual process of consciousness what is rejected as false is also part of the true. The false has content (par. 39). True and false are relative determinations dependent upon their position in the development of the experience of consciousness.

Hegel says: "In speculative [*begreifenden*] thinking, as we have already shown, the negative belongs to the content itself, and is the *positive*, both as the *immanent* movement and determination of the content, and as the whole of this process. Looked at as a result, what emerges from this process is the *determinate* negative which is consequently a positive content as well" (par. 59). What is the speculative sentence upon which the doctrines of dialectical inversion and determinate negation and, in general, the experience of consciousness depend? Hegel describes it in musical terms. The distinction between subject and predicate that exists in the general form of a proposition "is destroyed by the speculative proposition" (par. 61). He says the conflict between the general form of the subject and predicate and the unity produced between them by its transformation into true conceptual form is like "the conflict that occurs in rhythm between metre and accent. Rhythm results from the floating centre and the unification of the two" (ibid.). Hegel says that in the speculative or philosophical proposition the unity of the subject and predicate is meant to emerge as a harmony, that is, the subject is not simply dissolved into the predicate or the reverse.

Putting this in general terms, Hegel says that in speculative thinking the passive subject of reflective thinking or *raisonnement* perishes in an active relation with its object and "enters into the differences and the content, and constitutes the determinateness" (par. 60). Picture-thinking (*Vorstellung*), Hegel says, also cannot cope with this disappearance of the subject into its predicates. *Vorstellung* normally is a way of thinking that runs through predicates in order to get beyond them. But it discovers that "the predicate is really the substance, the subject has passed over into the predicate" (ibid.). Although *Vorstellung*, unlike *raisonnement*, is a holistic way of thinking, it is unable to go further because the subject cannot be located and has disappeared into the predicates. *Vorstellung* suffers from not being a truly dialectical way of thinking. It can only *present* the subject as its predicates, so to speak.

Hegel explains the speculative sentence in paragraph sixty-two, which deserves to be read several times. He uses the example: "God is being." God, the subject, in order to be what it is, is taken up or dissolved into the predicate, "being." What God is, after all, is "being." That is the meaning of the proposition. But as "being," God, as a definite subject, so to speak, ceases to be. We are taken back to God as the subject to determine exactly what the predicate is. Hegel explains this circular motion a second time, with the example: "The *actual* is the *universal*." We move from subject to predicate to subject again. The crucial point is that on the return to subject we do not possess the same subject. It has been affected by the process of the movement, because now it is a subject that stands as something determined by its predicate. Hegel says: "Thinking therefore loses the firm objective basis it had in the subject when, in the predicate, it is thrown back on to the subject, and when, in the predicate, it does not return into itself, but into the subject of the content" (par. 62).

Hegel's point concerning the difference between reflection and speculation can be seen from their Latin roots. *Reflexio* (*reflectere*) is "to bend back," "to turn back or reverse." *Specio* (*specere*) is "to spy out," "to see into." In the general form of the proposition typical of reflective thinking, the subject moves to the predicate and is thought simply to turn back to the subject. No dialectical change has occurred. In the speculative proposition, in the movement from the subject into the predicate, something has been "seen into" about the nature of the subject such that as it returns, keeping the predicate in relation to itself, it is no longer the same as the original subject. Upon this sense of thinking Hegel's *Phenomenology* depends.

In summary, reflection in the service of the understanding allows us to experience the world commonsensically, as a world of particular things that can be brought together into various orders of things and various levels of these orders. For the understanding the knower is separate from the known. The knower, through the power of reflection, can grasp the known. Reflection allows us to "understand" the world. The hallmark of this understanding is that the knower regards the object it knows as having a reality other than its own reality. Reflection begins to be in the service of reason when the knower turns its reflective activity away from the reality of the world as something other than itself and attempts to use reflection as the means to have access to its own reality. The knower attempts to reflect on itself, not on what it takes to be other than itself. This self-reflection is the step that consciousness requires in order to transpose reflection into speculation and to allow the understanding to be superseded by reason.

The phenomenon of self-reflection suggests to the knower that all knowing, including knowledge of the object, may be apprehended as a kind of self-knowledge. The knower's self-knowledge is not separate from the object as known. Speculation stems from this sense of self-reflection. Consciousness enters into speculation when it realizes that what it knows of itself cannot be divorced from what it knows of the object. Reflection when turned backward onto the knower becomes self-reflection, and when self-reflection is extended back onto the self's relation to the object, speculation is born for consciousness. In a wider sense, speculation has been there all along and was presupposed by reflection. Once consciousness, in its drive toward knowing, is in possession of the speculative moment, it can experience all knowing as a kind of self-knowing.

CHAPTER 2

Hegel's "Introduction": The Double *Ansich*

Hegel did not give a title to the approximately one dozen pages now called the "Introduction" to the *Phenomenology*. In the original they stand as simply some opening pages, and near their end Hegel says the *Phenomenology* is the "science of the *experience of consciousness*" (par. 88). The science proper begins with the first stage of "Consciousness," that is, "Sense-certainty." In the preface Hegel gives us a phenomenology of philosophical consciousness broadly drawn, directed to the reader who may hold the positions he describes: the critical philosopher of subjective idealism; the absolute idealist whose dialectic is based on the principle of identity; the romantic philosopher of edification and enthusiasm; the Enlightenment adherent to argumentation or *raisonnement*; the rationalist advocate of mathematical method as a model for a science of spirit; and the common-sense thinker who cannot pass beyond appearance, appealing to "an oracle within his breast" to solve philosophical problems.

The preface also addresses the reader who believes in prefaces, that is, the belief that a subject matter can be known prior to and apart from thought entering into the world of the subject matter, on the subject matter's own terms. Hegel satirizes those philosophers who, "in order to keep up with the times, and with advances in philosophy, read reviews of philosophical works, perhaps even read their prefaces and first paragraphs" (par. 70). Hegel abuses in advance the professional philosopher, saying that such readers blame the author if they cannot understand a work, speaking of the noiseless action of "these dead men when they bury their dead" (par. 71). Hegel says comprehension of his work requires a rare individual who can overcome his own concerns and achieve the level of true science.

In the dozen pages of introduction Hegel gives us a second set of phenomenological comments. If the preface is, broadly speaking, a phenomenology of the reader, these pages of introduction are a phenomenology of the phenomenon. By this I mean Hegel presents the reader with an account of consciousness itself as a phenomenon. He says what, in general, consciousness is.

In the preface he has defined consciousness as "the immediate existence of spirit" that "contains the two moments of knowing" (par. 36). In the preface, as in the introduction, Hegel defines "experience" (*Erfahrung*) as the movement of consciousness between those two moments of knowing that consciousness exercises on itself (pars. 36 and 86). In the introduction Hegel presents the reader with the shape of the general phenomenon of consciousness, apart from any specific content. This general shape, characterized by the polarity of its two moments, will be recognizable in the particular shapes of consciousness as we follow its pathway toward its final shape as absolute knowing. In the introduction we see the shape of consciousness itself. In the rest of the *Phenomenology* we will see this shape as it enters into the various contents or stages of consciousness.

Hegel presents the phenomenon of consciousness in the second half of the introduction (pars. 81–89). In the first half (pars. 73–80) he discusses the phenomenon of cognition (*Erkenntnis*). His organizing image is the "fear of error," which he opposes to the "light of truth" (pars. 73–74). Hegel's question is: What should be the starting point of science? Science wishes to know the true itself, the absolute. How can we avoid error? Whether cognition is seen as an instrument or as a medium, the problem is the same. Science can attempt to determine what form it must take to avoid error, in advance of engaging in the actual production of knowledge, or science can simply begin and see if it can produce knowledge, treating the problem of error as it goes. The first of these choices is that taken by Locke and, especially, by Kant.

Kant is the frightened philosopher. His fear of error leads him into critique, to try to establish the perfect conditions under which philosophy or cognition can function. He is the philosopher of prolegomena, concerned to delineate the basis from which philosophy or scientific cognition can think. In ordinary experience the fear of error is what leads us to try to establish whether we can actually do what we can do, before we do it. The fear of error is a deep impulse in one type of philosophical mind. The outcome of this drive to prolegomena, to the avoidance of error in philosophy, Hegel says, is always the conclusion that cognition cannot secure a knowledge of what exists in itself.

Hegel has in mind Kant's restriction of cognition to the phenomenal object and the separation of it from the thing-in-itself (*Ding-an-sich*). Hegel says: "This feeling of uneasiness is surely bound to be transformed into the conviction that the whole project of securing for consciousness through cognition what exists in itself is absurd, and that there is a boundary between cognition and the absolute that completely separates them" (par. 73). Since its inception, Kant's account of knowledge has faced the grand embarrassment, if not the grand deception, that we can know only what the object is for us, that what it is in itself cannot be known.

Kant asks that we grant this one distinction and promises that if we do, then all else can be epistemologically perfect. We can discover the necessary principles of cognition of the object as a phenomenon for the knower. Then we can proceed, with the luxury of advancing all sorts of creative views of what the world is like in itself, as Kant does in the *Third Critique*, maintaining the sweeping distinction of what is *constitutive* versus what may be considered *regulative* of the object. If we hold to this program as rigorously as Kant does, we can be free of the fear of error. Of course, the thing-in-itself is there and will not go away. We know about it in some important sense because we continue to talk about it, even within the confines of Kantian philosophy.

Hegel asks: "Should we not be concerned as to whether this fear of error is not just the error itself?" (par. 74). He says:

"Above all, it presupposes that the absolute stands on one side and cognition on the other, independent and separated from it, and yet is something real; or in other words, it presupposes that cognition which, since it is excluded from the absolute, is surely outside of the truth as well, is nevertheless true, an assumption whereby what calls itself fear of error reveals itself rather as fear of the truth" (par. 74). Kantianism is an early form of analytic philosophy; it is a process of making distinctions that goes on until a framework of limitations is established within which all the distinctions work; that is, until they all are mutually supportive. But what of the "light of truth"? The true is the whole, not the part. If it is to be anything, Hegel holds, philosophy must attempt to see the real directly in terms of the light of truth. It must attempt to know the thing itself, the absolute, and to know in terms of the absolute all that is not absolute. Hegel says: "This conclusion stems from the fact that the absolute alone is true, or the truth alone is absolute" (par. 75).

Having abandoned the "fear of error," Hegel now can allow doubt and skepticism to enter into the search by consciousness for truth. He introduces this through a second image, "the highway of doubt or despair" (*der Weg des Zweifels* or *der Verzweiflung*). Hegel intends this to be a real pathway of doubt, as distinct from the doubt undertaken in order to convert doubt immediately into certainty. He gives a one-sentence description of Descartes' doubt, this road of doubt or despair: "For what happens on it is not what is ordinarily understood when the word 'doubt' is used: shilly-shallying about this or that presumed truth, followed by a return to that truth again, after the doubt has been appropriately dispelled—so that at the end of the process the matter is taken to be what it was in the first place" (par. 78). Descartes offers no causal account of the true. Through his method of doubt he simply stamps as certain the basic tenets we hold at the beginning of his inquiry—that the thinker exists, that God exists, and that the world exists. Nothing beyond the relief of the fear of error has been gained by the guarantee of certainty.

Skepticism in Hegel's sense is not directed to doubt of particular propositions or beliefs. It is skepticism directed to whether any truth can be found in the phenomenal world at all. All may be illusion. Hegel's science of the experience of consciousness prepares the reader to answer Descartes' question of the evil genius. Of the type of skepticism he intends, Hegel says, "The skepticism that is directed against the whole range of phenomenal consciousness, on the other hand, renders the spirit for the first time competent to examine what truth is" (par. 78). The discovery of illusion enters the pathway of the stages of the education of consciousness at every point. Each stage of consciousness appears to consciousness as holding the principle necessary for the science of spirit. But as consciousness attempts to grasp and develop the shape of this principle at any stage, the form of knowing it has discovered dissolves into illusion before its eyes. Out of this illusion, consciousness necessarily assumes a new shape and its education continues toward its goal of absolute knowing, toward a grasp of the self-determined whole. Skepticism, like reflection, is subsumed within the process of speculative thought. Each is turned against itself in order to grasp the thing itself. Like common sense, both are inverted; each is made to walk on its head. The evil genius is forced to prove its own existence and in so doing dissolves its powers.

In the second half of the introduction (pars. 81ff.), Hegel offers his method, or what he calls the "presupposition which can serve as its underlying *criterion*" (par. 81). This criterion of true knowing is internal to consciousness itself. Hegel says: "Consciousness provides its own criterion from within itself, so that the investigation becomes a comparison of consciousness with itself" (par. 84). From this criterion Hegel will derive both his conception of experience and his conception of necessity, that is, all that is required for his science in general. We must give these statements of Hegel our closest attention to be certain we understand them. If we do not grasp them, we will be mistaken about what is taking place at every stage of the *Phenomenology*, and since they contain the nature of Hegel's conception of dialectic, we will be confused about the internal order of Hegel's whole system as developed in the *Science of Logic* and other works.

What Hegel actually says, in these few pages, is not what he has often been taken to have said. The major errors of misinterpretation of Hegel by his commentators comprise a list as long as the catalog of ships in the second book of the *Iliad*, and I do not intend to enter into them in any extensive way. In the end one must read the book for oneself. Present in the room should be only Hegel and the reader. Forget the interpretations; they are an excuse for not absorbing the text originally on one's own. No one can become a philosopher who worries about comparing interpretations or keeping up with recent views. One might become a scholar this way, or an expert, but not a philosopher. This said, I wish to call attention to two commonly heard views concerning Hegel's "criterion." One is that Hegel has a dialectic of thesis-antithesis-synthesis, or something like this three-step movement. The other, related to this claim, concerns Hegel's use of the German verb *aufheben* (sub. *Aufhebung*) as a doctrine of synthesis.

No first-rate Hegel scholar speaks of Hegel having a dialectic of thesis-antithesis-synthesis. In 1958 Gustav Müller, in an article, "The Hegel Legend of Thesis, Antithesis, Synthesis," pointed out that Hegel never uses these three terms together to describe the dialectic. As mentioned above, Hegel attributes triadic form to Kant as a lifeless schema (par. 50). Müller asks how this legend of the Hegelian triad came about, since it is not something one would naturally conclude directly from Hegel's text. He traces the likely origin to some lectures given several times by Heinrich Moritz Chalybäus, who shortly after Hegel's death interpreted the "new philosophy" using the triadic formulation from Kantian and Fichtean philosophy. He gave these lectures on one occasion in Berlin, at which time, Müller says, Karl Marx may have been present, as a student. But the myth persists, conveyed to students in survey courses in the history of philosophy. It is commonly held, both within and outside the field of philosophy, by those who have only a second- or third-hand awareness of Hegel.

Beyond this specific, historical origin, the triadic form of Hegel's dialectic is often embraced by those who have approached Hegel's system in the reverse of its own course of development. The most accessible work of Hegel is the *Encyclopaedia of Philosophical Sciences in Outline*. This has three parts: the logic, philosophy of nature, and philosophy of spirit, and the subdivisions of these parts are also triadic. Many British Idealist interpreters have approached Hegel's system from the *Encyclopaedia*. The book of W. T. Stace, *The Philosophy of Hegel: A Systematic Exposition*, is rigidly based on this, making it a work of easy access to Hegel for generations of English-reading students. It must be kept in mind that Hegel wrote the *Encyclopaedia* as a handbook for teaching philosophy to young students. It presupposes the dialectic of consciousness in the *Phenomenology*, in which philosophical knowing is itself generated for the philosopher. The *Encyclopaedia* presupposes Hegel, the philosopher of his own system, present, as the guide to what is meant, and directing the student who is listening to his oral amplifications of the text.

The triadic conception of Hegel's dialectic has been closely interwoven with his use of *aufheben*. *Aufheben* has been a doctrine of great importance for those who have a more sophisticated version of the dialectic than the mechanism of thesis-antithesis-synthesis. *Aufheben* is an untranslatable German verb made from the ordinary verb in German, meaning "to raise," or "raise up," "lift up"—*heben*, with the prefix *auf*. *Aufheben* is often translated in Hegelian works as "to sublate"; in Miller's translation it is rendered as "supersede" (*Aufhebung*, "sublation"). *Aufheben* can mean two things at once: "to cancel or transcend" and "to preserve." It is in this double sense that Hegel most often uses it. How seriously are we to take Hegel's use of *aufheben*?

Many commentators have taken it very seriously and have found in it a doctrine of how one stage of consciousness originates from the next on the pathway toward the absolute. This has produced what I will call the "snowball" theory of the absolute. Some recent writers on Hegel, such as John H. Smith in *The Spirit and Its Letter*, have suggested that we have taken *aufheben* too seriously, and that it has an ironic connotation in the *Phenomenology*. This is an interesting suggestion, and it fits with Hegel's general use of the trope of irony in the

Phenomenology. The ironic interpretation fits with the fact that in the *Phenomenology* one stage of consciousness seems just to collapse, and consciousness jumps straight to the next stage. There is no clear sense of progression or transformation, no sublation. The *Phenomenology* is in essence a scene of ironic juxtapositions that lead up to absolute knowing.

The snowball theory regards the *Phenomenology*, and Hegel's system as a whole, as a progression of forms in which each stage is taken up into the next and preserved in its differentiations. Like a snowball rolled across a lawn, it starts small and gets bigger and bigger until, in this view of Hegel's stages, we have a whole. The snowball theory is strong on the preservation or "taking up" meaning of *aufheben*. The ironic view does more justice to the sense of cancellation and transcendence. The ironic view is certainly more interesting, and likely closer to a true reading of Hegel's text. Hegel's dialectical juxtapositions, like those in an ironic statement, are based on the power of human wit or *ingenium*, an ability well-known to the Renaissance humanists but lost to modern thinkers who, from Descartes on, approach thought in terms of method.

Ingenium (ingenuity, wit) is the ability to see a connection between two seemingly diverse things. It lies behind the creation of hypotheses in the sciences and behind the tropes of metaphor and irony in the poetical and rhetorical use of language. Necessity is the mother of invention, and invention depends upon the power of *ingenium* to see new connections. Ingenium cannot be taught as such. It is unlike method, which can be taught. *Ingenium* may be grasped and developed through examples, but it is not subject to theoretical instruction. Hegel's dialectical method, like Socratic method, is not properly a method. Dialectic is a direct exercise of *ingenium* to connect diverse moments of experience. Hegel and Socrates show how this can be done. Once Hegel's dialectic is seen as an exercise of *ingenium* and not as a peculiar form of deduction, the reader can relax and set about to see what Hegel sees.

What does Hegel say the criterion that consciousness carries within itself is? His statement of it is extremely clear and carefully drawn (esp. pars. 85–87). I will call attention to some of its basic features.

1. It concerns the *in-itself* (*Ansich*) and the way the in-itself is taken up as a moment within consciousness.
2. It concerns *two* moments as Hegel describes it, not three. Hegel speaks of these two moments as *entsprechend*, as answering to each other in accord, or as *gleich*, as alike, proportionate. Consciousness never unifies them or synthesizes them. It holds them together only as inseparable moments of itself.
3. Hegel's most important statements of this are as follows, and probably should be committed to memory:
   (a) "But the distinction between the in-itself and knowledge is already present in the very fact that consciousness knows an object at all. Something is *for it* the *in-itself*; and knowledge, or the being of the object for consciousness, is, *for it*, another moment. Upon this distinction, which is present as a fact, the examination rests [*Auf dieser Unterscheidung, welche vorhanden ist, beruht die Prüfung*]" (par. 85).
   (b) "Consciousness knows *something*; this object is the essence or the *in-itself*; but it is also for consciousness the in-itself. This is where the ambiguity of this truth enters. We see that consciousness now has two objects: one is the first *in-itself*, the second is the *being-for-consciousness of this in-itself*" (par. 86).
4. What it means for consciousness to have *experience* is to pass from the first to the second of these moments.
5. These are two completely distinct moments. One cannot be collapsed into the other, yet nothing separates them. We might apply here Hegel's comments on the *void* as a principle of motion, which he discusses favorably in the preface (par. 37). There is a *void* between the two moments. They are not held together by a specifiable relation or connection. They simply *stand* to each other. The fact that, for either to be at all the other must be, expresses exactly what is meant by *necessity*. Their distinctness yet mutuality of existence is the basis of Hegel's claim that the progression of the forms of consciousness is *necessary*.
6. Consciousness moves forward through its necessary progression, apprehending the object by the doubling of the in-itself.

The in-itself as an object *for consciousness* now becomes a new in-itself that becomes a further object for consciousness, and so on. In this way consciousness acquires experience and develops toward the standpoint of the whole or absolute knowing.

7. There is one further dimension of this process of consciousness, and that is what this process is *for us*, the "we" (*wir*) that have somehow already undergone this process and are now witnessing it as a necessary sequence. For we who witness this process, we have an apprehension of consciousness as it is in-itself and as it is for-itself. We can comprehend to ourselves both moments as *in-and-for-itself*. We have the perspective of the "and." Hegel says: "But it is just this necessity itself, or the *origination* of the new object, that presents itself to consciousness without its understanding how this happens, which proceeds for us, as it were, behind the back of consciousness. Thus in the movement of consciousness there occurs a moment of *being-in-itself* or *being-for-us* which is not present to the consciousness comprehended in the experience itself" (par. 87).

These seven aspects of the criterion carried within consciousness in its apprehension of its object can be comprehended in a more holistic manner. Consciousness has experience by placing itself at odds with itself. It divides itself into two moments. One moment is the simple act of knowing or apprehending something that seems to be before it. The other is the immediately subsequent self-awareness that it has engaged in this act. In ordinary terms: I know, and, I know that I know. Consciousness is a "twone." Consciousness is one but it is a one that meets itself in this double sense. When consciousness steps back from its first moment to its second, the second moment becomes a new first moment from which it can now step back. I wish to call this sense of the two first moments the double *Ansich*, the double in-itself. Consciousness doubles up. Experience is this process of the movement of consciousness against itself. The internal motion of consciousness captured in these two moments is not a pendulum. Its internal motion is not a simple back-and-forth oscillation. The twoness formed in each passage from one moment to the other generates a further sense of twoness, a new sense of the world that presupposes the sense of the world of the previous twoness. This dialectic of pairs of moments is the sense of time that functions within consciousness.

There is even a larger principle of twoness that prevails between this temporal process of the increasing comprehension of consciousness of itself and the whole of consciousness that is the ever-present reality in which this temporality occurs. The temporality of consciousness is the pursuit of this wholeness. The two ultimate senses of consciousness, as a process and as a whole, is what Hegel intends to capture in his metaphor of the revel in which all participants are collapsing into each other, producing ever-new configurations of activity, but, as he says, apprehended from afar, as a whole, it is just as much a scene of transparent, unbroken calm (par. 47). Consciousness always finds itself paradoxically at both of these standpoints at once, never able fully to join itself in its specific forms of activity with its sense of the oneness of itself as a whole.

CHAPTER 3

Hegel's Reason: A Digression

According to Hegel, philosophical thought can engage in either reason or understanding. Understanding is essentially an activity of making distinctions and labeling. It is Hegel's contents-mentality—experience as a skeleton with tickets stuck all over it. Reason is the process of speculation; it occurs through the formulation of speculative sentences in which subject and predicate are folded back on themselves. The aim of speculation is to penetrate the inner life of the object and to capture in thought the intrinsic movement of the object. Thus every object is in truth a subject. The life of a subject is caught up in the life of all things. The life of reason allows the mind's eye to see into the inner illumination of the object. The understanding has no interest in the inner life of the object. The understanding is concerned with the object only to the extent that it can reflect its own powers off the object and thus know it.

Descartes and Locke are the first philosophers of reflection. Locke, in *An Essay Concerning Human Understanding*, is the first to use "reflection" in the philosophical sense in English. Locke distinguishes two sources of our ideas. One is sensation, the means by which we experience objects. The other source of ideas is the experience our own mind has of its operations. This is internal sense; the other is external sense. Locke says: "But as I call the other Sensation, so I call this REFLECTION, the ideas it affords being such only as the mind gets by reflecting on its own operations with in itself" (I: 123–24).

In a letter to Antoine Arnauld, on July 29, 1648, Descartes writes: "We make a distinction between direct and reflective thoughts corresponding to the distinction we make between direct and reflective vision, one depending on the first impact of the rays and the other on the second." Descartes says the simple thoughts of infants are direct and not reflective, such as when they have feelings of pain or pleasure originating in the body. "But when an adult feels something, and simultaneously perceives that he has not felt it before, I call this second perception *reflection* [*hanc secundam perceptionem reflexionem appello*], and attribute it to the intellect alone, in spite of its being so linked to sensation that the two occur together and appear to be indistinguishable from each other." In this passage Descartes draws the analogy that is the basis of the modern conception of reflection. He compares the reflection of light in perception, the subject of optics, with reflection in the intellect, the subject of mental philosophy. The historical source for reflection in French is the *Discourse* (1637), where Descartes uses reflection in parts 4 and 5. I have given an account of the history of reflection and its connection to the development of the science of optics in *Philosophy and the Return to Self-Knowledge.*

The understanding, in its distinctive marking and labeling, ignores time except as Kant conceives it—as one of the forms of intuition. The understanding attempts to achieve necessity in its formation of experience by ignoring time as a feature of the real. Hegel's reason, in contrast, is a way of realizing the nature of time as part of the inner life of the object become subject. To think dialectically is to bring reason into time, into the actual movement of experience. Dialectical thought takes the knower into the movement of experience and imitates it, in the sense of directly capturing this movement in language.

To bring reason into time is always in some sense to make the process of reasoning a narrative process. Narrative is the natural form of temporal thinking. There is no narrative of the present or the future; the narrative always connects the past remembered to the present or the future. The art of the narrative is the art of the Muses who, as Hesiod says, could sing of what was, is, and is to come (*Th.* 36–39). The art of the Muses is the basis of reason, in Hegel's sense. The original product of the Muses is not philosophy but the fable, the work of the poets. As Joyce says: "Fabled by the daughters of memory. And yet it was in some way if not as memory fabled it" (*Ulysses*, I, 24).

Once reason becomes the form of time it becomes a form of memory. What kind of memory is reason? Reason is not simple narrative, nor is it chronology. As history, reason is the comprehensive form of philology; that is, of the deeds, words, laws, and customs of nations at war and in peace. As philosophy, that is, as wisdom loved, it is what Hegel calls *Erinnerung*, or recollection. Recollection is distinct from ordinary memory.

To remember is to live in time. In his short treatise *On Memory* Aristotle says: "The object of memory is the past. All memory, therefore, implies a time elapsed; consequently only those animals which perceive time remember, and the organ whereby they perceive time is also that whereby they remember" (449b27–30). The human animal both has a power over time and is in time. Aristotle says, in the *History of Animals*: "Many animals have memory, and are capable of instruction; but no other creature except man can recall the past at will" (488b25–26). To remember in a human sense is to be able to recall the past at will, to know that one was born and has lived through time. To remember is to have memories, and further, to employ them as a basis of education and practical life.

Aristotle says, in *On Memory*: "If asked, of which among the parts of the soul memory is a function, we reply: manifestly of that part to which imagination [*phantasia*] also appertains; and all objects of which there is imagination are in themselves objects of memory" (450a21–23). Both memory and imagination originate in sense perception: "As to the question of which of the faculties within us memory is a function, it has been shown that it is a function of the primary faculty of sense-perception, i.e., of that faculty whereby we perceive time" (451a17–19).

Memory depends upon the power of the imagination to form sense perceptions of things into images in which it alters or imitates them. Both memory and imagination are active forces. In the *Topics* Aristotle says: "Perception is a state, whereas movement is an activity . . . for memory is never a state, but rather an activity" (125b17–19). In the *Posterior Analytics* he says: "So from perception there comes memory, as we call it, and from memory (when it occurs often in connection with the same thing), experience; for memories that are many in number form a single experience" (100a3–6).

Imagination is the way memory in its activity fixes and retains the sense perception. The imagination is an active force. This is evidenced by the fact that imagination can be employed by the poet in the act of making. Through the power of the imagination the poet makes metaphors. Plato understands *phantasia* in the *Theatetus* as a blend of judgment and perception (195D). In the *De anima* Aristotle understands it as intermediary between perceiving (*aisthēsis*) and thinking (*noēsis*) (427b–29a). Cicero says that it is an "impulse from the outside" that can be grasped by the soul (*Acad. post.* I.11.40–42). Aristotle says: "Imagination must be a movement resulting from an actual exercise of a power of sense. As sight is the most highly developed sense, the name *phantasia* (imagination) has been formed from *phaos* (light) because it is not possible to see without light" (*De an.* 429a1–4).

Francis Bacon states in *Sylva Sylvarum*: "Imagination, is of three kinds: the first joined with belief of that which is to come: the second joined with memory of that which is past: and the third is of things present, or as if they were present." The song of the Muses, with its three moments of time, suggests from the beginning that memory in its full capacity is not simply recalling past impressions, or remembering things. Memory in its fullest sense is recollection. This means that the things remembered and formed by the imagination must be put into a proper order.

A song has an order; like a narrative, it has a beginning, middle, and end. Aristotle says, in *On Memory*: "When one wishes to recollect, that is what he will do: he will try to obtain a beginning of movement whose sequel shall be the movement which he desires to reawaken. This explains why attempts at recollection succeed soonest and best when they start from a beginning" (451b29–32). To recollect requires the location of the beginning of a thing and the formation of it in the mind as it develops from its past to the present and anticipates a future.

In *On Memory*, Aristotle distinguishes memory from recollection. Recollection implies memory, but not the reverse. He also distinguishes two types of recollection, "necessary and customary." "Acts of recollection occur when one impulse naturally succeeds another: now if the sequence is necessary, it is plain that whoever experiences one impulse will also experience the next; but if the sequence is not necessary, but customary, the second experience will normally follow" (451b).

Recollection requires a beginning and an ordering of its contents into a sequence from that beginning. Hegel says, in the final paragraph of the *Phenomenology*: "Spirit has to begin unbiased from its immediacy in this new world and move once more to maturity, as if all that preceded was lost and it had learned nothing from the experience of the earlier spirits. But the *re-collection* [*Er-innerung*] has preserved this and is the inner being, and, in fact, higher form of substance" (par. 808, my trans.).

The act of recollection, which is the act of reason, takes us within experience. In *An Essay on Man*, Cassirer says: "In man we cannot describe recollection as a simple return of an event, as a faint image or copy of former impressions. It is not simply a repetition but rather a rebirth of the past; it implies a creative and constructive process. It is not enough to pick up isolated data of our past experience; we must really *re-collect* them, we must organize and synthesize them, and assemble them into a focus of thought. It is this kind of recollection which gives us the characteristic human shape of memory, and distinguishes it from all other phenomena in animal or organic life" (p. 51).

Philosophical recollection, as opposed to historical or literary recollection, is causal ordering—knowledge *per causas*. It is not customary but necessary, in Aristotle's terms. Philosophical recollection, which is expressed in the sequence of speculative sentences, is dialectical order, and this order is necessary. What is narrated is a necessary order of events remembered. The art of the philosopher is to see, in time-remembered, a necessary order of things—to see how things could not have been otherwise. In this way the philosopher is a master of time. To master time is to find beginning points and to find the necessary sequence of order. It is the eye for the good infinity in which each thing in the sequence illuminates the other, in a light shown face to face.

In this way reason enters time, but time is always in dialectical opposition to a *Jenseits*, a beyond, what is beyond time at any point of beginning. Thus to set a beginning for recollection the philosopher is out of time. To pass back in thought to a place of beginning is to escape the sequence at that point. There is the *Jenseits*. In Hegel's term the *Jenseits* is the void between the in-itself and the in-itself-for-consciousness, what lies inside the *double Ansich*. Seeing inside the twoness of the *Ansich* is the moment of speculative beginning. Not to see this is to settle for the understanding, for reflection, or external knowing. Hegel is the artificer of dialectic, who escapes from the island of pure understanding, with its labyrinth of transcendental distinctions. We who would go with him must heed the warning not to go too near the direct light of the sun.

CHAPTER 4

Hegel's System: Dialectic of "Andness"

Hegel published four books, and posthumously there appeared the volumes of lectures on the philosophy of history, the history of philosophy, philosophy of art, and philosophy of religion. In addition there are early and miscellaneous writings. These make up Hegel's corpus. In the lectures, Hegel is inventing whole fields of study that have become the center of the humanities in the contemporary world. Except for the philosophy of history, the lectures present the historical material behind Hegel's divisions of absolute spirit: art, religion, and philosophy.

Hegel's little writings are interesting in themselves and in some instances provide insights into how his system came to be. There are Hegel's so-called *Differenzschrift*, on the difference between Johann Gottlieb Fichte's and Schelling's systems; *Glauben und Wissen*, Hegel's little treatise on faith and knowledge; the early theological writings; the fragment of a system of 1800; the fragment on love; the lesser political writings that have been collected in English by Z. A. Pelczynski; and the "Jena System," the system as Hegel first sketched it out, while teaching at Jena. There is also Hegel's correspondence, a good portion of which has been translated by Clark Butler in a large volume, *Hegel: The Letters*. The four volumes upon which Hegel's mature system rests are *Phenomenology of Spirit* (1807), *Science of Logic* (1812–16), *Encyclopaedia of Philosophical Sciences in Outline* (in the original and two revised versions—1817, 1827, 1830), and *Philosophy of Right*, published in 1821, ten years before Hegel's death.

The *Philosophy of Right* is an expansion of sections on forms of moral and political life from the *Philosophy of Spirit* of the *Encyclopaedia*. Both the *Philosophy of Right* and the whole of the *Encyclopaedia* contain *Zusätze* attached to each of their sections. Both of these works were written directly as textbooks and used in various periods of Hegel's teaching. The *Zusätze* are summaries of points, taken from Hegel's lectures, that amplify the original text. These four major books of his system were all closely connected with his teaching. In Jena he announced the *Phenomenology* as a course, prior to writing it, and the *Science of Logic* was connected to his teaching in Heidelberg. When Hegel was not lecturing on the history of philosophy, which he did throughout his career, or on other fields, he was teaching his own system directly.

What is the system? I wish to give a basic overview of its paradoxes and possible general order. One thing is clear: Hegel conceived the system as having two parts—the phenomenology or the doctrine of appearance, showing the ways in which phenomena are known, and the science of logic or the doctrine of the real idea, showing the forms of metaphysical or categoreal knowledge. The "science of the experience of consciousness" results in the "science of logic." By "logic" Hegel means, not logic as an organon or instrument of thought, but metaphysics—logic as the rational form of the actual. At the beginning of the *Science of Logic* Hegel says that the categories, which are the subject matter of the *Logic*, are nothing more than what is already present in language. In this Hegel is following Aristotle, in that the categories are the most universal predicates, but he does not accept Aristotle's notion of the organon.

At the end of the section on sense-certainty in the *Phenomenology* Hegel writes of the "divine nature" of language, which is its power to take thought to the universal. Hegel understands language as the embodiment of rationality in regard to this power. Any language is implicitly a logic and hence a metaphysics. Language itself as the form of spirit is the power to grasp the actual in thought, to form it as the idea. Ordinary logic, that taught to philosophy students and as the instrument needed to think well in all fields of inquiry, focuses only on certain aspects of language and how these can be used to guide thought in its formal endeavors, the forms of the proposition, the syllogism, logical analogy, etc. These are subsumed within Hegel's full sense of logic and are explicitly treated in the *Science of Logic*.

Hegel is clear, in the preface to the *Phenomenology*, which falls between the completion of that work and the *Science of Logic*, that the forms of spirit of the *Phenomenology* lead up to the *Logic*. He says: "Their movement, which organizes itself in this element into a whole, is *logic* or *speculative philosophy*" (par. 37). At the beginning of the *Science of Logic* Hegel reiterates this connection. In the title page of the original edition, Hegel designates the *Phenomenology* as "System of science, first part." Until the *Phenomenology* was given attention by French commentators such as Jean Hyppolite and Alexandre Kojève it was regarded as an early work of Hegel, not important to the system, and it was not much read.

Findlay, in his foreword to the Miller translation, says that the *Phenomenology* is meant to be a "forepiece" to the system (which he identifies with that of the *Encyclopaedia*), "but it is meant to be a forepiece that can be dropped and discarded once the student, through deep immersion in its contents, has advanced through confusions and misunderstanding to the properly philosophical point of view" (p. v). Findlay has also called the *Phenomenology* an *auto-da-fé*, the burning of a heretic as ordered by the Inquisition. In other words, once the individual gets to the stage of absolute knowing and has properly comprehended everything, the ladder, which Hegel says the reader has a right to demand—that will take his own consciousness to the standpoint of the absolute—can be thrown away (par. 26).

At no point does Hegel clearly take so extreme a view of the disposal of the *Phenomenology* as does Findlay. In fact, he speaks of the need to read philosophical works many times (par. 63), although this comment in itself is not incompatible with Findlay's view. Presumably Findlay agrees that the *Phenomenology* must be read many times. The way Hegel speaks at the beginning of the *Science of Logic*, suggests that the *Phenomenology* needs to be kept in an active relationship to the second part of the system, perhaps in the way that the philosopher—thinking purely speculative thoughts and, in this sense, not living in the world the way others do—still lives in the world and does not exist apart from its appearances.

Hegel says his system is a circle. In the *Science of Logic* he says it is a circle of circles joined as a chain, a *Kette*. How are we to understand the first major link in this chain, that between the *Phenomenology* and the *Logic*? The key lies in the concept of the phenomenological observers, the "we," who are looking on as consciousness travels its highway of despair, moving from in-itself to the in-itself for consciousness, which becomes a new in-itself—the process of the double *Ansich*. As we observe consciousness move between its two moments, forging its progression of shapes, we see consciousness take the stance of *being-in-itself* and the *being-for-itself*. In so doing we develop our own grasp of what conscious experience is. Although inapparent to the consciousness that is undergoing the movement of experience, apparent to us is the fact that consciousness has being *in and for itself*. The key element here is the "andness" in the *in and for itself* that the phenomenological observer perceives but which remains below the surface and only implicit for the consciousness that is being observed.

If we were to call the in-itself a "thesis" and the for-itself an "antithesis," we could not go on to call the in- and for-itself a "synthesis." The constant conjunction of two moments is not a synthesis. Conjunction is not unification. Hegel could, but never does, write of a "being-in-for-itself" (*An-für-sich-sein*). He always states this as *An-und für sich sein*, as a conjunction: *und*, "and." The will-o'-the-wisp that consciousness pursues, in its acquisition of experience, is to experience *as a phenomenon* the synthesis or unity of its two moments. It enters into each of its shapes with this hope, and exits each one, having found its initial sense of a synthesis to be an illusion, only to try again the same process in different terms; that is, in terms of another phenomenal shape, which it now assumes. It is a process of hope and despair, consciousness often forgetting itself and having to begin all over again. The memory or process of recollection that provides consciousness with its moments of experience has within it an act of constant forgetting. This propensity to forget forces consciousness constantly into its "labor of the negative" (*Arbeit des Negativen*).

For the "we," what consciousness is for us, consciousness is a series of differently shaped conjunctions of itself, each one leading to the next, from the very simple illusions of synthetic unity in sense-certainty and perception at the beginning of the process, to the elaborately developed versions of spiritual life and the "last grand illusion" of religion, where the unity of all things seems nearly answered. But religion fails to bring forth the whole in a conceptually determinate way and the object and its essence remain conjoined only in *Vorstellung*. How does absolute knowing differ from all the other shapes of consciousness leading up to it? Is absolute knowing something that is achieved just by a final adjustment of the object and its essence to make them agree, or is it radically different, capable of canceling what has gone before as illusion?

Absolute knowing is the standpoint of philosophical wisdom or speculative knowing itself and it is where the "we," the so-called observers, and the consciousness undergoing experience merge. In fact the "we" has not been a pure observer with an independent standpoint; all along it has been affected by what it sees and its being changes, as David Parry has shown in *Hegel's Phenomenology of the "We."* The standpoint of absolute knowing is the realization that there is no synthesis of the two moments of knowing in the phenomenal realm. It is the realization and acceptance that the "and" is truly there; that it remains as actual.

Free of the illusion of synthesis, yet with all these senses of it in mind, held there through the power of "recollection" (*Erinnerung*), consciousness goes forth as thought and enters the *Science of Logic*. The *Science of Logic* asks the question: Given that there is no phenomenon of synthesis, can synthesis be successful as thought, as a direct possession of reason itself? The *Science of Logic* is a discourse on the possible meaning of "and." Each category is a thought that can possibly bring together the two moments of being-in-itself and being-for-itself. The first category is what they fundamentally share: being.

This is why the *Science of Logic* begins with being rather than nothing. "Andness" is something, not nothing. "From nothing, nothing comes" (*Ex nihilo, nihilo fit*). Being shares with nothing the universality of indeterminateness, and in its passage toward nothing and back, the category of becoming emerges.

The beginning of the *Science of Logic* is based on the "speculative sentence"—"Being is Nothing." Nothing as predicate of being expresses its indeterminateness, but once we are at nothing we are driven back to being, then to the movement itself, or becoming (*Werden*). Without connecting the beginning of the *Logic* to the "speculative sentence" of the preface of the *Phenomenology* (written as a bridge to the *Science of Logic*), we cannot understand why the *Logic* begins as it does, and we may become inclined to hold all sorts of views.

Because what exists between the in-itself and the for-itself is a void, no phenomenal sense of a relation between them can be found. Thought attempts, in the *Logic*, to turn what was the mere conjunction between the in-itself and the for-itself into a specifiable relationship that is expressible as a category of thought. Thus the *Logic* moves from being to becoming to quality, quantity, measure (*Das Mass*), and so forth, on through all possible categories of thought, each category encountering intellectual difficulties in realizing the whole. The final thought is the "absolute idea," which Hegel, in a well-known problematic passage, says "freely goes forth" as nature (*Selbst frei entlässt*). The absolute idea bifurcates itself into nature and then into spirit. Here we enter into the *Encyclopaedia*, which has three parts, a summary of the *Science of Logic* known as the "Lesser Logic," the *Philosophy of Nature*, and the *Philosophy of Spirit.*

How can the idea become nature? How can thought become nature? It does not. It becomes the idea of nature—that is, it becomes the philosophy of nature—the speculative comprehension of the internal order of nature. How does it freely go forth? What is the nature of the transition? This has mystified those who hold to a nonironic, strict conception of *Aufhebung*, in which, at every turn, the system must make a smooth recapitualization of itself, a flawless dialectic of deductive stages. The solution, in a word, is that the idea can go forth freely as nature because consciousness earlier entered the logic by freely going forth as thought. The phenomenology stands to the logic as in-itself stands to for-itself. They are conjoined by a void. The idea stands to the idea of nature, and later, of spirit, as in-itself stands to for-itself. They are also conjoined by a void. Hegel's use of the chain as his image of the circle of the system is apt; it is precise.

Each part of the system, whatever that part is taken to be, is a circle linked to another circle, the succeeding part of the system. The form of their joining is a link. The links are not fused; there always remains a gap, the space at which they touch. "Andness" is what is struggled with throughout the system, first as consciousness, then as thought, then as the "andness" that philosophy tries to bridge between nature and spirit. But further, the "andness" is struggled with within the system itself, for it is there at each and all of its links. It is with "andness" or the conjunction of the void with which the philosopher is constantly trying to live. The true is the whole and the whole is always not yet. We cannot go too near the sun.

I want to say a final word about the status of the *Encyclopaedia of Philosophical Sciences in Outline.* It is clearly a pedagogical work, a textbook. The summary presentation that it contains of the *Larger Logic* has some fine moments, but it is nothing like the *Larger Logic* in regard to the amount of philosophy that it contains. The *Larger* or *Science of Logic* is full of digressions, the classic form in which the most vital philosophical ideas are conveyed. Hegel may have brought some of this manner of digression to the *Lesser* or *Encyclopaedia Logic* as he employed it in his lectures. The *Philosophy of Spirit* contains some of the material from the *Phenomenology* in a section so titled, but in a restricted form. The *Phenomenology* and the *Science of Logic* are not books that can be taught; they must be self-taught. They can be learned only in an autodidactical fashion. The *Encyclopaedia* can be lectured from. The system can be taught from it, but is it the real system, or does the real system lie behind it, in the *Phenomenology* and *Science of Logic*, that from which Hegel was actually speaking when he lectured?

To answer this, the title of Hegel's textbook needs to be considered carefully: it is an "encyclopaedia" and it is an "outline." It is something for the public. It is an answer to the Encyclopaedists (Denis Diderot and d'Alembert) and to the skeptical Pierre Bayle, author of *The Historical and Critical Dictionary*. The works of the Encyclopaedists are collections of scientific understandings, but they are not scientific, for they are not systematic. Hegel's *Encyclopaedia* shows the power of his conception of philosophy to give the public a synoptic of knowledge and not simply a critique of its various forms. The sources for Hegel's thought are not simply the standard works in the history of philosophy. They go back into the esoteric ideas of Renaissance Neoplatonism and the theosophical mysticism of Jacob Böhme, as shown by Glenn A. Magee in *Hegel and the Hermetic Tradition* and by Daniel H. Fernald in *Spirit's Philosophical Bildung*. As John H. Smith has shown in *The Spirit and Its Letter*, Hegel was closely in touch with the classical and German rhetorical traditions.

The *Encyclopaedia* is a handbook, "Hegel made easy." One can learn, with some diligence, what it has to say but—where is the highway of despair? Where are the intricate digressions of the speculations of the greater logic? What I would say of the *Encyclopaedia* is less true of the *Philosophy of Right*, even though it is a magnification of some of the stages of the *Philosophy of Spirit* of the *Encyclopaedia*. The *Philosophy of Right*, with its famous preface, is more vital, agile. It takes the reader into the best Hegel has to offer on moral and political questions. It takes the reader back to the spirit of the *Phenomenology* and is a work that deserves to be more discussed, in relation to what is said in the *Phenomenology*, but to do so with profit requires first a good grasp of the *Phenomenology* and the *Science of Logic*.

A final word concerning irony and the dialectic of Hegel's system: Irony is the distinctively philosophic trope. It is originally tied to the question of self knowledge by Socrates—"Socratic irony"—in which it is also connected with dialectical thinking. Irony is deliberately saying other than what one means, usually saying the opposite of what is meant. Why not simply say what is literally meant? Why reverse what is meant into an irony? If I say "they are all, all honorable men," something more is said, beyond simply declaring them to be dishonorable men. Any ironic statement is inherently dialectical. It requires us to play one meaning against another, to play what is said against what we see as meant—that is, if we get the irony. The two moments of the irony allow something to be said that is more than could be captured in the literal declaration. Giambattista Vico, in his discussion of "poetic logic" in the *New Science*, says irony is the philosophic trope (par. 408). The thought-form of the myth is metaphorical, but never ironic. When the philosophers arrive in history, they introduce their trope of irony into thought.

The irony forces us to make the true meaning of the statement for ourselves. Irony, as a trope of philosophical expression, mirrors in its two moments the "doubleness" that is inherent in consciousness—its double *Ansich*. The irony occurs from the side of the for-itself and directs our attention back to the in-itself, forcing us to hold the two moments together as in- and for-itself. The joints of Hegel's system have this ironic structure. We seem never to state them successfully as a literal principle of transition. *Aufhebung*, even at these large moments, keeps its ironic tension, canceling and preserving. Literal-mindedness in philosophy is always a mistake; it flattens out the real. Early in his career Hegel warned against those whom he calls *unsere Buchstabenphilosophen* (our literal-minded philosophers). As with Socratic thinking so with Hegelian thinking: we must look for the irony. Hegel explains that he intends *aufheben* to have these two senses of preservation and negation, operating together in his definition of *aufheben* in the section of sense-certainty (par. 113). His irony always brings out what the subject is in itself.

CHAPTER 5

The Beginning of the *Phenomenology*

What is the beginning of the *Phenomenology*? Hegel says "our object cannot be anything else but immediate knowledge itself, a knowledge of the immediate or of what simply *is*" (par. 90). He says it is "sense-certainty" (*Die sinnliche Gewissheit*). What kind of certainty is it? It is certainty of "this," "I, *this* particular I, am certain of *this* particular thing" (par. 91). The truth of sense-certainty, he says, is to be just that I am and that the thing is. Consciousness is certain of both as such, but not because either is grasped as the result of any process of mediation. Does Hegel intend this as a picture of how human consciousness first comes into the world? Is this a description of the first terms of its experience?

As mentioned above, Hegel claims the *Phenomenology* provides the reader with a ladder to climb from the most rudimentary forms of experience to the highest (par. 26). It provides the means by which both consciousness and the reader may make this ascent. Can we understand this beginning point of sense-certainty in anthropological terms, as the beginning of human consciousness itself? Or is it to be understood as the beginning of that form of consciousness that has, however dimly, taken on the question of truth that has already within it an impulse toward absolute knowing? If it is the latter, then the beginning of the *Phenomenology* is intended as the beginning of philosophical consciousness, not of human consciousness in general.

In the second volume of the *Philosophy of Symbolic Forms*, the volume on *Mythical Thought*, Ernst Cassirer says that he wishes to take Hegel's ladder of the *Phenomenology* a step lower. He says Hegel begins his experience of consciousness at the level of the thing and its attributes and the thing as distinct from the I. Cassirer maintains that experience begins in a world of mythical forces and energies, before consciousness senses the object and the I as discrete thisness and as heres and nows. Hegel's world of sense-certainty is a world of proto-common sense, which becomes a world of ordinary common sense (*gesunder Menschenverstand*) as it evolves toward the end of the account of perception (*Wahrnehmung*). Cassirer claims that before consciousness engages in acts of sense-certainty it experiences the world as *felt*.

In his phenomenology of knowledge (*Erkenntnis*), the third volume of his work on symbolic form, Cassirer calls this the *Ausdrucksphänomen*—the "phenomenon of expression." The world is first felt, as a scene of benign and malignant forces, which are expressed in myths. The first world of consciousness is not a world of neutral "heres" and "nows" but one of gods and demons, light and dark, sacred and profane. The "I" is not a distinct "this" but is part of the immediate flow of sensation. As the "I" develops a separation from the object, it experiences the other as a "thou," not as a thing or a pure "this." What Cassirer says in general is supported by anthropologists, such as Claude Lévi-Strauss, depth psychologists, such as C. G. Jung, historians of religion, such as Mircea Eliade, and developmental psychologists, such as Jean Piaget. In the life of the individual human it is clear that children feel and express the world before they engage in acts comparable to sense-certainty, such as Hegel describes.

Cassirer is indebted to Hegel in many ways, including his view of the "dialectic of mythical consciousness," in which the mythical develops toward the world of representation determined by the *Darstellungsfunktion* of consciousness, in which consciousness achieves from the immediacy of the expressive function the power of commonsensical and referential forms of language and symbolism. Cassirer develops his own metaphysics from his view of mythical thought in accordance with his own version of Hegel's dictum that the true is the whole, as Thora Bayer has shown in her discussion of the "basis phenomenon" of *Werk* in *Cassirer's Metaphysics of Symbolic Forms*.

Could Hegel, in the early nineteenth century, have considered mythic thought in these terms? Could he have begun his ladder at a lower level? Cassirer regards his philosophy of mythical thought as having only two basic sources: Vico's *Scienza nuova* (*New Science*) and Schelling's *Philosophie der Mythologie*. He claims that Vico is the "real discoverer of the myth" (*der eigenliche Entdecker des Mythos*). Vico wrote in the eighteenth century, but there is no evidence Hegel read Vico. Schelling's views on myth are involved with his conception of religion that is a part of his idealism. Anthropology as we know it did not exist in the early nineteenth century. J. G. Frazer's *Golden Bough* and E. B. Tylor's *Primitive Culture* are products of the end of that century and the beginning of the twentieth. But thought about myth is very old; the details can be found in Burton Feldman and Robert D. Richardson, *The Rise of Modern Mythology 1680–1860*. The eighteenth century had thought a great deal about the savage mind and about other cultures. Frank Manuel, in *The Eighteenth Century Confronts the Gods*, states there was a common insight that the thought of contemporary savages, peasants, children, and archaic cultures was the same.

It is entirely possible that Hegel could have formulated a philosophy of mythology as a conception of original mentality, apart from what he says in relation to religion, because Vico did it. There is nothing like Vico's "poetic wisdom" (*la sapienza poetica*) in Hegel. Hegel seems never to have made his own discovery of the myth, having discovered nearly everything else about the human world. Yet in his conception of the development of spirit he made the modern study of anthropology largely possible, along with many of the historically based social sciences.

Hegel's consciousness of sense-certainty is not a conception of the point at which mind or spirit itself is formed. It already contains a distinction between "I" and object and it is already in possession of language. The eighteenth century was fascinated with the origin of language—one has only to think of Jean-Jacques Rousseau's *Essay on the Origin of Languages*—and Hegel provides no account of the origin of language in human consciousness. Language is already there, as a force that moves sense-certainty toward the universal. As we read this section we sense that sense-certainty is answering more than the question of what the world is. That is the question, so to speak, that mythical thought answers with its formation of the world as gods and the divisions of it into sacred and profane times, spaces, and numbers. The universal that is present in language in sense-certainty is not Vico's "imaginative universal" (*universale fantastico*) of mythos but the essentially rational universal of logos. The phenomenon of sense-certainty is not simply that of having a world but of how the world is known. It is the first attempt by consciousness to face the question of knowledge.

The beginning of the *Phenomenology*, then, is the moment in consciousness when philosophical consciousness begins. The ladder Hegel provides is the ladder the individual may climb within consciousness in general to achieve philosophical knowing. Hegel's book is not a book for everyone; it is a book for those who would become philosophers. The reader comes to the book *in medias res*, that is, the reader is already at some rung of the ladder. Hegel takes the reader back to the original skeptical moment, the moment of uneasiness and uncertainty, to which sense-certainty is the most immediate answer. The reader is then brought forward, up and past where the individual reader's consciousness was, at first coming to the book, and is drawn on to the comprehension of absolute knowing. If the reader can ascend with the stages of the book, to its summit, the wisdom of absolute knowing will be grasped, but many will be unable to complete the full journey. Hegel's book is a book for philosophers, a book on the self-knowledge of the philosophical life.

What, then, is sense-certainty? It must be a tacit awareness of skepticism, an uneasiness, a skepticism about the object that consciousness attempts immediately to allay by claiming the "I" and the object to be unquestionably a "this." Consciousness does not know what it is doing; it is only trying to stay within the firmness of the immediate. As the phenomenological observers, we can see that sense-certainty is the most primitive reaction possible in thought to skepticism. Without question, I am this and the object I know is this. Whatever they are, my senses tell me at least that they *are*. I am a sentient being and I can sense immediately what is. But as I attempt to maintain the being, unity, and simplicity of "thisness," it begins to dissolve.

As Hegel has promised, skepticism enters into consciousness from the beginning. It is answered only by "staring the negative in the face" (par. 32), by a doctrine of determinate negation. Consciousness at the stage of sense-certainty is just beginning to learn this. Determinate negation is Hegel's principle that in the logic of actual experience there is no null class, as there is in ordinary logic. To affirm something is at the same time to negate all else. What is negative has content. It is something; it is not nothing. As the double "this" begins to dissolve into the multiplicity of the "heres" and "nows," consciousness begins to tarry with the negative. Consciousness cannot hold on to one moment, for to do so it must divide itself into the moment per se and its holding of the moment as part of itself.

What happens to consciousness in sense-certainty? Part of the key to this is Hegel's pun on *Meinen* and *mein*. *Meinen* in German is equivalent to the seldom-used English infinitive "to opine," to have an opinion. A common German expression is "*Meine Meinung ist* . . . [My opinion or 'meaning' is . . .]." Hegel begins the problem of the *Phenomenology* with the question of truth and knowledge as it enters modern philosophy, as the quest for certainty. The ghost of Descartes is with us throughout the stages of "Consciousness" into "Self-consciousness" (the "truth of self-certainty") and into "Reason" ("the certainty and truth of reason"), which recalls the latter part of Descartes' title of the *Discourse*: "rightly conducting reason and of seeking the truth in the sciences." Consciousness here is not seeking truth as a knowledge *per causas*: it is seeking instead the preliminary assurance of what is certain.

Hegel makes the Cartesian shift from seeking certainty in the sense-object to seeking certainty in the "I." He says: "The certainty is now to be found in the opposite element viz. in knowing, which previously was the unessential element. Its truth is in the object as *my* object, or in its being *mine* [*Meinen*]; it is because *I* know it" (par. 100). This is not Descartes' *cogito* because it is still a process of being certain on the level of what can be sensed. It is not quite solipsism, because consciousness at this level is not that sophisticated. The pun forecasts the drive by the "I" to possess the object that we will see emerge as active desire (*Begierde*), at the level of self-consciousness, with the master-servant relation, in which the object becomes another self or "I."

Consciousness attempts to get at the particular by circumventing language through the act of pointing, or "ostensive definition." But this leads to a multiple of "heres" and "nows," as did the attempt earlier to designate the particular by writing it down (par. 95). Finally Hegel says, to those who seek certainty in the sensed particular, what "is meant *cannot be reached* by language, which belongs to consciousness, i.e. to that which is inherently universal" (par. 110). They should learn the mysteries of Ceres and Bacchus, of eating bread and drinking wine, namely, that particulars are not solid things of sense. Animals show this wisdom of the potential nullity of particulars by falling to and eating particulars up. Particulars can be eaten, digested, interacted with, but they cannot be thought.

Our attempts to think the particular cause us to affirm only that most universal of universals—the "this," or "what is," "being." Any attempt at immediate knowing of the immediate fails. Hegel points out that natural consciousness often learns from experience what is true in it "but equally it is always forgetting it and starting the movement all over again" (par. 109). Consciousness now decides to settle for a version of its object that is had through the senses but which is mediated; that is, a multiplicity held together in some way.

Hegel introduces the section on perception by another pun. He says: "instead of knowing something immediate I take the truth of it, or *perceive* it" (par. 110). Hegel's play is on the German for "to perceive," or *wahrnehmen*. His wordplay is on the prefix *wahr*, "true," and *nehmen*, "to take." "*Ich nehme es wahr*," "I take it true," "I perceive it." Consciousness now attempts to take the object truly, to accept the object and knowledge as involving the universal. But as Hegel's title of this section indicates, the appearance of the thing as involving the universal also involves the active presence of deception. At the level of sensation there is a struggle for the certainty of immediacy, but it is naive. At the level of perception the object begins to be formed as a thing by the act of knowing, and with this type of knowing, deception enters.

Deception can enter consciousness at this early a stage in experience because Hegel understands perception to be a kind of judgment or proto-judgment rather than a passive reaction of the senses. To take something for true means also that something has been selectively excluded. Perception, like judgment at the level of thought, affirms something as true, while excluding all that is not affirmed as false. Deception enters because consciousness acts as if no act of exclusion is involved in its affirmation of its object. It pretends to itself that everything is simply there in the world to be perceived. The world is a collection of things.

There is a further sense of deception that adheres to the stage of perception; this involves the fact that the thing has a nonperceptual dimension. The senses in the act of perception grasp the thing in terms of its various properties. Thus the thing is perceived as having a particular color, and also as having a particular shape, and also as having a particular kind of surface, and so on. All these properties are claimed to inhere in the thing itself, which is not accessible to sense perception. Consciousness at the stage of perception acts as if all that is required for its object to be a thing is derived from perception. But in fact the perceptible thing is a consequence of a ground that is not in principle perceptible. The deception, the attempt to act as if all that is true of the world derives from the senses, leads consciousness from perception to the nonperceptible element or essence, which is claimed to be what holds the thing's properties together. This nonperceptible sense of the thing is a product of the understanding. Thus consciousness is led beyond perception as the sole basis of experience.

The skepticism that is tacitly presupposed at the beginning of the *Phenomenology* is for the first time beginning to have a visible affect. By playing on the word *wahrnehmen*, Hegel calls attention to the fact that perception is a kind of "judgment" made by the senses. It is a short step from forming the object by the senses to forming it by the understanding. Thus the understanding is present as a shadow from the start of perception. Deception is present because if I take something for true, there is the possibility I can take it falsely. What I take for true can be in fact false.

The act of the animals in sense-certainty, of eating the particulars, shows the true sense of the particular being mine. By my eating it, the particular becomes me; it is mine. It is not mine in the form of an opinion or a "meaning"; it is actually mine. When consciousness takes the object for true or perceives it, it assumes that the object is there as a thing, a universal; the disappearance to sense of any particular instance of the thing would not make the thing itself disappear as a certain kind of thing. To eat some blades of grass is, so to speak, not to eat the thing: grass. The problem for consciousness is to know the unity of the thing. The thing becomes, first, the "also" that holds all its various properties together, which are themselves universals, white, cubical, and so on. From this we move to a distinction of primary and secondary qualities (par. 119). The thing remains a unity, a one, and we, the knowers, become the universal medium in which the properties inhere.

This sense of the thing as a medium creates the problem of how the thing itself maintains its determinateness from other things. The problem is how the thing can be a one-in-many, have a relation to itself, yet have relations to other things. The thing then is conceived as being what it is "insofar as" it has such-and-such properties. How the determinateness of the perceptual thing is to be formulated moves back and forth from the thing to the I.

This process culminates in "perceptual understanding" or "sound common sense." Common sense oscillates between holding that things are just what they are, independent of us, and saying that things are also what we think they are. This perceptual understanding or common sense fails to arrive at any truth it can consistently state about the world. It shows its own untruth, however, in trying to maintain its position while reducing all things in experience to their abstract universal characteristics.

CHAPTER 6

Force, Understanding, and the Inverted World

The section on "Force and the Understanding" is one of the most difficult in the *Phenomenology*. In his foreword to the Miller translation, Findlay claims that, try as he will, he has never grasped all of its dialectic (p. xiii). It may simply be impenetrable in regard to all its specifics. It is a crucial section, since, as we have seen from the preface, Hegel wishes to oppose the understanding (*Verstand*) to reason (*Vernunft*). Here he wishes to present the understanding as the summary stage of all of consciousness. Consciousness, as the first major part of the *Phenomenology*, develops through three stages: sensation, perception, and understanding. Hegel's dialectic moves through substage after substage, which correspond to the actual inner movements of consciousness as it attempts to realize its truth of the object. Is there a way to step back from these particular dialectical transformations, to see what Hegel is presenting in general? Without some overview we cannot very well hold in mind the process and its goals. We can construct this backward, beginning with the nature of the understanding.

Near the middle of "Force and the Understanding," Hegel says: "*Our object* is thus from now on the syllogism which has for its extremes the inner being of Things and the Understanding, and for its middle term, appearance" (par. 145). If we write out Hegel's syllogism, it is this:

> B-A The inner being of things is distinct from the appearance of things.
> U-A The understanding of things is distinct from the appearance of things.
>
> ---
>
> U-B The understanding of things is distinct from the inner being of things.

Although on first glance, appearance as the middle term would seem to relate the understanding to things, this relationship falls apart at each joint of the syllogism, because we must begin with the fact that the appearance is distinct from the thing-in-itself. The syllogism is an AAA-2 and is invalid, as it fails to distribute its middle term. Hegel says, however: "The inner world, or supersensible beyond, has, however, *come into being*; it *comes from* the world of appearance which has mediated it; in other words, appearance is its essence and, in fact, its filling" (par. 147). The problem for consciousness, at this moment, is how to grasp the mediation of appearance in a positive sense.

Hegel makes clear that this syllogism in itself is Kant's position in the critical philosophy. The understanding knows appearance but has no knowledge of the thing-in-itself. But of course once the thing-in-itself is distinguished from appearance it *comes into being*, as Hegel says above. As Hegel says, the Kantian standpoint is one of positing the thing-in-itself, as a pure beyond, a *Jenseits*. It is completely empty; it is the nothingness of appearance. Hegel says: "even reveries are better than its own emptiness" (par. 146). The understanding cuts us off from the inner being of things and so turns its back on reason, just as Kantian philosophy does. What is the route that consciousness has come, in general, to this phenomenon of appearance as the object of the understanding?

The struggle we have been witnessing is the birth of the universal. In fact, it is the birth of the "concrete universal," the *Begriff* (in Miller's terms, the "Notion"). The *Begriff* has within it the sense of grasping not present in the English "concept," which derives from Latin *conceptus*. *Begreifen* is from *greifen*, to grasp. (*Griff*, for example, is a handle of a tool.) To think conceptually, then, is to grasp the object in thought. With his sense of *Begriff*, Hegel is attempting philosophically to grasp what is concrete, to think the particular in the universal, or literally to think the individual. This is a conception of organic form, the kind of "subjective universality" that Kant explores in the *Third Critique* but which, according to his critical principles, he cannot claim to be constitutive of the object.

Consciousness, then, attempts to "think" or "grasp" the concrete particular directly through the senses, at the level of sense-certainty. It is unable to do this because a "this" is the universal of universals. The particular will not stand still but is transformed into the universal "here" or "now." But the universal will not stand still, either, for these universals are not a unity in themselves; they fall immediately into multiplicity, into "heres" and "nows." Consciousness attempts to take the object for true, to perceive (*wahrnehmen*) it. In so doing it turns the object into a thing, because the "here" is a universal and is composed of a multiple of "heres" we arrive at the object as a thing with properties, all of which are universals.

As mentioned in Chapter 5, the problem becomes the classic one, of how the properties of the thing inhere in the thing and make it truly what it is. Consciousness is attempting to solve this question in the only way it knows how—on the phenomenal level. It is seeking the phenomenon that can be perceived, which unites the thing as substance with its properties. Unable to do this via the distinction of primary and secondary qualities, it focuses attention back on the thing as having an inner movement. It regards the thing now as a "play of forces." The thing is a unity in the sense that it is a dynamic field of forces. But the questions remain: What is force? How is the play of forces also force? The solution is to allow the thing to retreat into itself as a force and to configure the play of forces as appearance whose action can be the subject of the understanding. The understanding can discover and state the laws of this activity.

In appearance as a middle term of the understanding and the thing itself, consciousness believes it has discovered as a phenomenon the "and" that joins the in-itself with the for-itself. This discovery is short-lived because it is bought at the price of knowing what the thing really is. The supersensible world of the thing itself may be what we expect it to be, from what the understanding can know from the appearance—or it may not. The possibility of a second supersensible world arises that is the inversion of the first (*die verkherte Welt*). The North Pole may in reality be the South Pole, and so forth (see par.

158). We cannot tell. Since we cannot know how things really are, they may be the inverse of what we would think them to be. There is no perception of the thing-in-itself to allow us to decide. We are at the threshold of Descartes' evil genius or anti-God who could deceive us systematically. The understanding can offer no solution based on its knowledge of the object of what it has uncovered—the phenomenon of inversion.

From the stage of sense-certainty onward, consciousness has had difficulty with the self. Consciousness apprehends the self at first as another "this." The self has been treated, throughout the whole stage of consciousness, as not different in principle from the object. Consciousness seeks a single way of knowing that can encompass the object and the self. In Kantian terms, the most the self becomes is the "I think" that is appended to the process of knowing the phenomenal object. With the failure of the syllogism of appearance and the emergence of the phenomenon of inversion, consciousness becomes desperate and realizes that it must either go on this way or give up the version it has of itself, as simply being "consciousness." Its solution is basically Cartesian: consciousness looks from the object back to itself. Thus it finds the self as an unexplained factor different *in kind* from the object. In this moment self-consciousness is born. It appears that in the reality of the self the problem of the "and" in the "in- and for-itself" is solved. Hegel says: "I distinguish myself from myself, and in so doing I am directly aware that what is distinguished from myself is not different [from me]" (par. 164).

The solution to the problem of the inverted world is that whether the thing-in-itself is the North or the South Pole, they both appear to me, the knowing self. Throughout the process of inversion I am a constant. It has been a mistake to attempt to penetrate the inner being of things through a doctrine of the object. The inner being of at least one thing, that is, the self, is there immediately to be had. The inner of the self is not closed to the self. The self can find no principle to justify with certainty that what it takes the world to be at any time is how the world really is. It is tormented by the thought that no matter how carefully it has perceived and understood the things of the world, it is possible that in reality all is different than it thinks, even that all is precisely the opposite. Consciousness cannot demonstrate that what seems to be the case, actually is the case. Nor can it show how what seems to be is related to and distinguished from what is. The solution to this metaphysical problem is for the knower or self to realize that all this uncertainty resides in itself. It can be certain of one thing, namely, that it is.

On the last page of this section Hegel uses a theatrical metaphor. He says: "This curtain [of appearance] hanging before the inner world is therefore drawn away, and we have the inner being [the 'I'] gazing into the inner world—the vision of the undifferentiated selfsame being, which repels itself from itself, posits itself as an inner being containing different moments, but for which equally these moments are immediately *not* different—*self-consciousness*" (par. 165). The term Hegel uses for curtain is *Vorhang*, a stage curtain. I have discussed in *Hegel's Recollection* the sense in which this image of the inverted world derives from Ludwig Tieck's play by the same name. Consciousness must go backstage, behind appearance; suddenly the curtain is lifted and there the "I" is standing, just as is the protagonist in Tieck's play.

Tieck published *Die verkehrte Welt* in 1799. He spent the winter of 1799–1800 at Jena, just prior to when Hegel arrived there in 1801, to assume his first teaching post, and, in the years that followed, to write the *Phenomenology*. The play was highly controversial; it reminds the contemporary reader of the theater of the existentialists of the mid-twentieth century. The play begins with an epilogue and ends with a prologue. There is a fictive audience on stage, watching a play on a fictive stage. In the play its characters can exchange roles with the fictive audience. The audience cannot always tell the difference between what is fiction and what is real. The play is so complicated it is difficult to determine what is to be understood as real and what is to be regarded as unreal. In the final speech of the play, one of its main characters says that he is the only person here (a kind of version of the existentialists' "last man"), and says that this fact needs to be investigated by the philosophers. The parallel with Hegel's metaphor of the I behind the stage curtain is striking.

In the latter part of the passage quoted above, Hegel says that the process of inversion is in effect taken on, into the being of the self. The self is a being that is selfsame yet "repels itself from itself." This principle of inversion that destroys consciousness as the ultimate form of experience, in particular, the understanding, is transformed into the principle of the inner life of the self. Consciousness through its preoccupation with the object has all along attempted to stop or avoid dialectic. Now the principle of dialectic—the passing of a moment to its opposite—is overtly taken up as the life of self-consciousness.

Dialectic is not a threat to self-consciousness but its security. The principle of inversion ceases to be perverse and becomes a positive force. In the inverted world Hegel has brought forth within his phenomenology the principle that is at the very basis of his conception of dialectic. The question now becomes: How does the self attain a knowledge of its own innerness? It is not difficult to see why the *Phenomenology* has been likened to a *Bildungsroman*, a novel dedicated to presenting the spiritual education of its main character. We now can observe the education of the self, and in the process the philosophical readers, the "we," will educate ourselves.

CHAPTER 7

Self-Consciousness of Masterhood and Servitude

The section on "Lordship and Bondsman" or "master-servant," as it is often called, is perhaps the easiest to read and understand in the whole of the *Phenomenology*. Everyone has something to say about it. We are very familiar with the kind of struggle of selves of which Hegel speaks, from Marxism, on the one hand, with its conceptions of alienation and labor, and from psychology, on the other, with its conceptions of loneliness and dominance. We are also familiar with it from Friedrich Nietzsche, existentialism, and contemporary phenomenology of the self. All these contexts allow us to look back on the original things Hegel is saying and find them to be familiar. It is a difficult section to interpret because the twentieth century itself has already interpreted it.

I wish to call attention to an interpretation of this section that is not to be found in the standard commentaries—the extent to which Hegel intends the bondsman or "servant" to be a portrait of philosophical consciousness, of the origination of philosophical selfhood. The explicit evidence for this is that the stages that immediately emerge from the success of the servant over the master are philosophical life-positions: stoicism, skepticism, and the unhappy consciousness. Stoicism and skepticism are well-known forms of philosophical selfhood, and the ironic term "unhappy consciousness" refers to the experience of the self as a form of finitude, another philosophical theme. Furthermore, when Hegel declares what the servant or bondsman achieves as the result of his labor, he says: "The bondsman realizes that it is precisely in his work wherein he seemed to have only an alienated existence that he acquires a mind of his own" (par. 196).

The product of the labor is not a physical acquisition but a particular mental achievement, "a mind of his own." Hegel says: "Having a 'mind of one's own' is self-will, a freedom which is still enmeshed in servitude" (par. 196). This is said at the end of the master-servant section and in his reflection on it at the beginning of the following section. Hegel says: "We are in the presence of self-consciousness in a new shape, a consciousness which, as the infinitude of consciousness or as its own pure movement, is aware of itself as essential being, a being which *thinks* or is a free self-consciousness" (par. 197).

The self in its struggle with the master is made into a being that *thinks*. Hegel points out that "*to think* does not mean to be an *abstract* 'I', but an 'I' which has at the same time the significance of *intrinsic* being" (par. 197). Hegel refers to two philosophical figures as examples of stoicism—Marcus Aurelius and Epictetus—"whether on the throne or in chains" (par. 199). Stoicism is a life-form but it is also a specifically philosophical life-form. If we look back from the stoicism section to the master-servant section, Hegel's intention begins to look rather different than if we consider the master-servant section by itself, as so many commentators do, taking it for their own purposes. Shortsightedness leads to distortion.

The above is some explicit evidence for considering the hypothesis that the servant is the beginning of the philosophical self, but the larger, implicit reason concerns Hegel's whole case. If the *Phenomenology* begins at the point consciousness feels the first urge of wisdom and attempts to answer skepticism with certainty, then what we are observing is the pathway of consciousness to philosophy, namely, to absolute knowing. We are not just observing the development of the forms of human consciousness as such. Within them we are seeing the emergence of the absolute, the achievement of a science of thought. The product of the labor of the servant is the freedom of the self that thinks. Hegel puts this in philosophical terms by saying that thinking is not the abstract "I think" attached to judgments, but a form of being.

How does this freedom of the self as thought come about? Hegel's title is "Herrschaft und Knechtschaft." The *Herr* is the "sir," the "master"; "-schaft" is "-ship," thus "mastership" or "lordship." The *Knecht* is the "servant," the one in servitude to another. The *Knecht* is not a slave (*der Sklave*). The *Knecht* is bound over in his whole existence to the *Herr*. He is not an ordinary employee, who can come and go as he wishes, but he is not a slave. It is a great mistake to call this the "master-slave" section, as many commentators do. Had Hegel intended this to be a dialectic of slavery he would have used the word, *der Sklave*. He discusses slavery as an institution in the *Philosophy of Right*. The phenomenon he is concerned with here is servitude. Independence from slavery is commonly gained through rebellion. Independence from servitude is gained through work. The relationship to the master is different for each. The slave has the status of property. The servant has the status of a self, although a self whose being is externally determined. The servant is dominated but not owned. Slavery and servitude involve two different logics that should not be confused.

In an age as psychological, psychoanalytic, and existential as ours, it is not difficult to go on at great length about the struggle of these two forms of selfhood in terms of the process of recognition (*Anerkennen*). Indeed, it is as though Hegel has declared the agenda of the twentieth century in distinguishing the moments of this process. But let us confine ourselves to what Hegel actually says about this, lest we just turn the unfamiliar into the familiar and then do with it whatever we wish. There seems to be no limit to what has been claimed in the name of Hegel's conception of "master-servant."

Having escaped from the syllogism of the middle term of appearance of the understanding, through the principle of the inverted world, to the "I" standing behind the curtain, consciousness has become self-consciousness. It has accomplished this only to find itself in a new syllogism in which it is the middle term of its own two extremes. Hegel says: "The middle term is self-consciousness which splits into the extremes" (par. 184). The difference is that the two extremes are versions of self-consciousness—unlike appearance, which was the problematic medium of the inner being of the thing, on the one hand, and the understanding, on the other. In this case Hegel says: "Each is for the other the middle term" (ibid.). "They *recognize* themselves as *mutually recognizing* one another" (ibid.). But as "extremes are opposed to one another, one being only *recognized*, the other only *recognizing*" (par. 185).

With the appearance of self-consciousness we have moved from the attempt by consciousness to answer skepticism with certainty, a certainty placed in the grasping of the object, to the attempt to answer skepticism by truth or, as Hegel puts it in his title, "the truth of self-certainty." To be certain of something is to remove all doubt. To know the truth of something is to bring forth its cause. The removal of doubt is neither knowledge nor truth. Knowledge or truth requires the adduction of cause. Without this difference fully in mind we cannot understand why these two selves or extremes of self-consciousness engage in a life-and-death struggle.

Hegel says: "Each is indeed certain of its own self, but not of the other, and therefore its own self-certainty still has no truth" (par. 186). Each self attempts to convert certainty of itself and uncertainty of the other into truth by demonstrating that it is the cause of the other. Hegel says: "In so far as it is the action of the *other*, each seeks the death of the other" (par. 187). Self-consciousness is a new play of forces within its own medium. The need to be the truth or cause of the other is the basis of desire (*Begierde*). To destroy the other is to be the other's cause.

To avoid this struggle of life and death is to decide to become nobody. Hegel says: "it is only through staking one's life that freedom is won. . . . The individual who has not risked his life may well be recognized as a *person*, but he has not attained to the truth of this recognition as an independent self-consciousness" (par. 187). A person, literally, in German, *Person*, is neither a *Herr* nor a *Knecht*. A *person* is not truly a self because a person has no inner being, no capacity for self-knowledge, which is the goal of spirit. Inner being can only be created through confrontation with the other. The life-and-death struggle is itself not the solution to selfhood either. Hegel says: "This trial by death, however, does away with the truth which was supposed to issue from it, and so, too, with the certainty of self generally" (par. 188).

The selves that survive the struggle survive as master and servant, and from the struggle a new form of mediation emerges that matches the earlier syllogism of self-consciousness and its extremes of recognized and recognizing. As the servant is bound up with thinghood, the master bonds the servant over to himself to mediate his desire for the independent thing (par. 190). The master dominates the thing by dominating the servant. This domination takes the form of the master directing the work of the servant in relation to the thing. Thus the master, freed of all the cares of work, can simply enjoy the thing. Hegel says: "For the lord, on the other hand, the *immediate* relation becomes through this mediation the sheer negation of the thing, or the enjoyment of it" (par. 190). He says that "what the bondsman does is really the action of the lord" (par. 191).

The lord rules the bondsman or servant by means of the constant recall of the fear of death. Fear is the result of the struggle that the lord appears to have won. But slowly the servant begins to recognize a basis of his own freedom in his work on the thing. He attains a moment of pure being-for-self. Hegel says: "This moment of pure being-for-self is also *explicit* for the bondsman, for in the lord it exists for him as his *object*" (par. 194). The lord is bound to the servant and the thing in order to achieve his enjoyment, but "through his service he [the servant] rids himself of his attachment to natural existence in every single detail; and gets rid of it by working on it" (ibid.).

The servant naturally develops stoicism through his work (*Arbeit*). This becomes his answer to fear, and fear is transferred to the lord, who experiences the anxiety of possibly losing his position of mastery. Hegel says that "the fear of the lord is indeed the beginning of wisdom," and that, through work, "the bondsman becomes conscious of what he truly is" (par. 195). Through work the negativity of desire is conquered. Hegel says: "Work, on the other hand, is desire held in check, fleetingness staved off; in other words work forms and shapes the thing" (par. 195). Desire can strive to control and enjoy the thing, but this can be achieved in only a momentary fashion.

The ability to work on the thing is actually to control it, to shape it in relation to the self.

This power of work is the secret the servant discovers and the master is unable to know. Hegel says the servant "becomes aware that being-for-self belongs to *him*, that he himself exists essentially and actually in his own right" (par. 196). If the servant were to remain fearful of the master, simply doing his bidding, the self would not develop. Hegel says: "Without the formative activity, fear remains inward and mute, and consciousness does not become explicitly *for itself*" (par. 196). The overcoming of fear through the confidence of work gives the servant "a mind of his own." In a sense the servant imitates the thing, in his independence, but it is an indcpendence of freedom because the independence is due not simply to a "thereness" but to a power of self-determination. The stoic, however, becomes a type of human thing, a life independent of all else.

What can we conclude, at this point, about Hegel's account of the master-servant? There is a principle of intellectual thought that doctrines should take their origin from that of the matters of which they treat. We may ask: What can be learned by the philosopher, the philosophical "we," from the dynamics of the master-servant? To understand itself, philosophy must discover its own nature, beginning with its origin. In the master-servant dialectic we see the origin of self-knowledge. It is essentially a Socratic picture. We see the relationship of philosophy as a work of the self placed in relationship to the power of the state, the *Herrschaft*. The Socratic philosopher must conquer the fear of the state in order to pursue philosophy. He is at the service of the *polis*, but it emerges that he is at this service on his own terms. The state or political power is always the *Herrschaft* that philosophy confronts; the state would have philosophy think its thoughts for it, and then step back to enjoy them. Yet the philosopher develops "a mind of his own."

The end of the Socratic drama historically is the triumph of the master and the death of its servant. But, as Hegel says, the point of the struggle is not for it to end in death (par. 188). In the fatal movement of consciousness the lesson philosophy has learned is to withdraw into stoicism. Philosophical consciousness exists, at its origin, in only a rudimentary form, and it can do little more. Thinking in the context of contemporary life, we children of Sigmund Freud, Marx, and existentialism tend, in this section, to seize on the conflict of the psyche and the struggle of the self and other as the core of this stage of self-consciousness. But if we understand it as the beginning, within consciousness, of not only self-consciousness but of philosophical consciousness proper, then Hegel has given an account of the basis of the question of self-knowledge. Self-knowledge is the question that lies at the basis of the *Phenomenology* and at the basis of philosophy itself—that sense of philosophy that Cicero said Socrates recalled from the heavens and brought into the cities and homes (*Tusc.* V.410–11).

In summary, the stage into which consciousness emerges from the master-servant is stoicism, followed by skepticism and the unhappy consciousness. The *Phenomenology* must always be read both forward and backward. The master-servant is such a powerful image of the human condition that we are tempted not to look closely at what emerges from it, and not to see these subsequent stages as keys to the subtext of the master-servant relationship itself. Since what emerge from the master-servant stage are stages of philosophic life-positions, we should consider whether the master-servant contains a general description of the philosopher's position in the world. Seen in this way, the master-servant becomes an instruction in practical wisdom (*phronēsis*) for the philosophic reader.

Philosophy since its origin has been in a problematic relationship to politics and political power. The philosopher does not command political power, for there are no actual philosopher-kings. The philosopher is in the servant position in relation to the state, because philosophy is subject to its power. Unlike the politician and those who are attracted to politics, the philosopher is a lover of wisdom—not a lover of honor or wealth, two achievements that are attached to economic and political process. The philosopher does not regard the state or the activity of politics as ultimate. Thus the philosopher is always a potential threat to the state. The philosopher lives *in* and needs the political order of the state, but the philosopher never is *of* it. The philosopher has a mind of his own that is based in the philosopher's connection to the world. Stoicism is philosophical servitude, a way to achieve independence while still living within the state. There is something stoical about every philosophical position—the sense that in it the philosopher is self-sufficient and that the philosopher's philosophy, whatever in particular it is, carries its own validity and truth that is beyond and untouchable by politics.

CHAPTER 8

Unhappy Consciousness

Through work, Hegel says, the servant acquires a "mind of his own." He says, "having 'a mind of one's own' is self-will" (par. 196). The servant, through his work, not only acquires skills and practical knowledge to supply his own needs and wants, which for the master can be supplied only by the servant; the servant acquires an intellect. The "freedom of self-consciousness" that emerges through the servant is based upon the powers of the thinking "I." This "I" or self attains its freedom in a negative way, by holding its own being apart from the world and from other selves. Hegel says that when this form of self-consciousness appears in the actual history of spirit it is called stoicism. He says: "Its principle is that consciousness is a being that *thinks*, and that consciousness holds something to be essentially important, or true and good only in so far as it *thinks* it to be such" (par. 198). He says: "As a universal form of the world-spirit, stoicism could only appear on the scene in a time of universal fear and bondage, but also a time of universal culture which had raised itself to the level of thought" (par. 199).

The stoic response to fear and the conditions of life under dominance is to assert independence. The stoic achieves self-knowledge through the reduction of all worldly needs to the thinking "I" that attaches itself only to the true and the good. Hegel says: "The true and the good, wisdom and virtue, the general terms beyond which stoicism cannot get, are therefore in a general way no doubt uplifting, but since they cannot in fact produce any expansion of the content, they soon become tedious" (par. 200). They become tedious because there is no civic dimension to them such as we see in the later forms of spirit itself. The stoic attains the certainty of himself by rejecting all else in the name of the highest ideals.

For the stoic, thought attains freedom by enclosing itself in its own circle. Stoicism is replaced in self-consciousness when thought becomes a power not just to transcend the world, but to consider its contents. Hegel says: "*Skepticism* is the realization of that of which stoicism was only the concept [*Begriff*], and is the actual experience of what the freedom of thought is" (par. 202). The skeptic asserts his independence or freedom of thought by examining and critically judging what is before the "I." The skeptic introduces a dialectic in that skepticism is a thought form that passes from one view to another. But in so doing, Hegel says, it is a "thoughtless rambling which passes back and forth from the one extreme of self-identical self-consciousness to the other extreme of the contingent consciousness that is both bewildered and bewildering" (par. 205).

The skeptic attempts to reject the world while at the same time holding on to it. Hegel says: "It affirms the nullity of seeing, hearing, etc., yet it is itself seeing, hearing, etc. It affirms the nullity of ethical principles, and lets its conduct be governed by these very principles" (ibid.). Hegel's portrait of the skeptic is the standard one, of the internal contradiction of the skeptical position of doubting, in thought, what the skeptic must accept in his own conduct in the world and in society. Hegel says: "Point out likeness or identity to it, and it will point out unlikeness or non-identity; and when it is now confronted with what it has just asserted, it turns round and points out likeness or identity" (ibid). He says this process of saying A and then B is "like the squabbling of self-willed children" (ibid.).

Hegel's portrait of the stoic, like that of the skeptic, is a conventional one. He emphasizes the stoic's withdrawal from the world and the skeptic's self-contradiction. But he aggressively attacks the skeptics, saying they are like squabbling children. Stoicism is an integral part of the philosopher's position in the world. Because the philosopher makes common sense walk on its head, the philosopher must have a distance from the world. The philosopher also shares with the stoic the dedication to the true and the good, wisdom and virtue. The stoic fails because in stoicism all of philosophy is reduced to withdrawal and the transcendence of the world, with these ideals.

How does Hegel's portrait of the skeptic relate to his comments on skepticism in the introduction (pars. 78–79)? He considers the *Phenomenology* as a pathway of doubt. He rejects the skepticism of Descartes as a mere method of thought that leaves us with only that with which we began. But he portrays skepticism as a crucial part of the education of consciousness to the level of science. He says: "The skepticism that is directed against the whole range of phenomenal consciousness, on the other hand, renders the spirit for the first time competent to examine what truth is" (par. 78).

The "science of the experience of consciousness" incorporates skepticism within itself as a continual aspect of the dialectical process that is answered only by the emergence of the whole. Nothing less than the concept of the true as the whole will answer serious skepticism. Skepticism is a natural attitude of the philosopher. As I have suggested, the attempt of consciousness to achieve certainty by the "this," "here," and "now" at the stage of sense-certainty is a response to the first feeling of consciousness of skepticism. Indeed, in the section on skepticism as a form of self-consciousness, Hegel says: "It [skepticism] exhibits the *dialectical movement* which Sense-certainty, Perception, and the Understanding each is" (par. 203). But skepticism taken up as the work of philosophy itself is "thoughtless rambling," no better than the bickering of self-willed children.

The skeptic, in other words, is a self-satisfied person who does not want his questions answered. Hegel's attack on skepticism illustrates the fact that consciousness can become frozen into any one of its forms along the pathway of its education and believe, mistakenly, that it has discovered the answer to what it seeks. In this case it believes that the answer to doubt, which is natural to the full process of truth, is to embrace doubt itself. The skeptic is an analog to the self that does not risk its being in the life-and-death struggle of the master and servant. The skeptic becomes a "philosophical *person*" but is unable to find the courage to pursue the love of wisdom to its end.

Self-consciousness as such is larger than its skeptical moment, and in its efforts to move out of the skeptic's dialectic of yes and no, it decides to accept its own dual nature. Hegel says: "In stoicism, self-consciousness is the simple freedom of itself. In skepticism, this freedom becomes a reality, negates the other side of determinate existence, but really duplicates *itself*, and now knows itself to be a duality" (par. 206). Skepticism leads directly to the "unhappy consciousness." Hegel says: "the *unhappy consciousness* is the consciousness of self as a dual-natured, merely contradictory being" (ibid.). Self-consciousness stops playing the game of the skeptic with itself and courageously accepts an "*unhappy, inwardly disrupted*" nature (par. 207). Over and against the contradictions of the skeptical stance, it posits the unchangeable: "The simple unchangeable, it takes to be the *essential* being; but the other, the protean changeable, it takes to be the unessential. The two are, for the unhappy consciousness, alien to one another" (par. 208).

Once these two realms are created, self-consciousness finds itself in an absurdity, because each is an other within the nature of self-consciousness itself. Yet they are opposites with no principle of connection. The term "unhappy consciousness" is somewhat misleading in English. Hegel's term is *unglückliches Bewußtsein*. Consciousness experiences an *Unglück*, a misfortune; it is not simply "unhappy." Being unhappy, in modern terms, can connote a psychological state in which we might adjust ourselves in some way to become content or happy. But consciousness finds itself in an objectively unfortunate condition, one that it cannot alter by changing its mental attitude. The unhappy consciousness is a philosophical state of existence like stoicism and skepticism. It is based on the first glimpse of the absolute, which is somehow part of its own self-knowledge or freedom, but it cannot fathom how it is such a part. The ultimate is cut off from it; it stops thinking and takes a religious attitude toward the unchangeable. Hegel says: "Its thinking as such is no more than the chaotic jingling of bells, or a mist of warm incense, a musical thinking that does not get as far as the concept [*Begriff*], which would be the sole, immanent objective mode of thought" (par. 217).

The unchangeable (*Unwandelbare*) is an individual and the consciousness that is the changeable is an individual, but it can find no way in thought to mediate these two. It "*finds* itself *desiring* and *working*" (par. 218) in the world but does not comprehend how to incorporate the unchangeable in this activity. In order to mediate these two poles of its existence, the unhappy consciousness finds a middle term, in the form of the priest. Hegel says: "This middle term is itself a conscious Being [the mediator], for it is an action which mediates consciousness as such" (par. 227). The price paid is that the self surrenders its freedom to this mediator, who then does all its thinking for it.

The solution is inadequate for the mediator also knows nothing. His mediation is not achieved by thought or the concept. The mediator or priest of the unchangeable becomes a second version of the master, now taking his claim to mastery not from his own power but from the incomprehensible unchangeable. The self indentured to the mediator now finds its way out by once again returning to the mind of its own, which now is reason. The true certainty of the self lies in the "certainty and truth of reason."

In this section Hegel broaches as a phenomenon a theme he develops conceptually in the *Science of Logic*—the "bad infinity" (*die schlechte Unendlichkeit*). The beyond or *Jenseits* of the unchangeable versus the changeable individual parallels the distinction between the infinite and finite of the metaphysics of substance. The unchangeable is a "bad," not "true" infinity because its reality is contingent on the reality of the finite. The unchangeable is not a truly independent existence. To be genuinely independent, a true infinity, it would need to be self-determinate. The infinity of its movement would need to be due to a principle internal to its being, not the result of its difference from another (finite) being. What at first appears to be a genuinely independent beyond turns out to be no more than a grand form of dependence, a second form of finitude inherent in self-consciousness.

Bad infinity, like the unchangeable beyond of the unhappy consciousness, is an inadequate concept of infinity. Infinity is the idea of that which is without any limits. The unchangeable is an inadequate form of infinity because it is limited in one crucial sense: the unchangeable is comprehensible only as distinct from the changeable. The unchangeable is limited because it is one term of an opposition. What the unchangeable is or ever can be is fixed by the sense in which it is not the changeable. The unhappiness of consciousness at this stage is due to the inability of consciousness to overcome the fixity of this opposition.

True infinity, as Hegel presents it in the *Science of Logic*, is the idea of the infinite as a principle of the self-development of the bond between the universal and the particular. One way to grasp what Hegel means by true infinity is to relate it to the idea of the functional order of a series, as Cassirer mentions in the third volume of the *Philosophy of Symbolic Forms* (pt. 3). If we consider φ as a variable representing a specifiable principle of order for a series of particulars, and x as a variable representing any unlimited order of a specifiable series of particulars such as a, b, c, d . . . , then φ(x) expresses a bond between universal and particular. The universal φ has no meaning apart from its role in determining the order of the series of particulars represented by x, and the particulars represented by x have no meaning apart from their place in the ordered series. Neither φ nor x has independent meaning.

The bond between φ(x) depends upon what Hegel calls true infinity. The x-series can be extended indefinitely, each next member of the series having a definite position in the series according to the principle of its construction present in the universal element, φ. Furthermore, φ may itself be a φ in another or meta-level series, just as any of the elements in the x-series may be a φ in relation to a subseries. The φ(x) can be infinitely self-developed in all directions, each step of development being determined and systematic. A visual example of this sense of infinity is to imagine a bottle with a label on it, the label being a picture of a bottle with a label on it, and so on.

The unhappy consciousness is an important stage in Hegel's *Phenomenology*, for it shows within Hegel's development of consciousness the nature of a false dialectic, a dialectic that can only pass back and forth between two poles that cannot be mediated. Any attempt to mediate it falls prey to what has been called the "third man argument." That is, if two things are to be related through a third thing, each of them requires a further thing to connect them to the third thing, and so on. An infinite regress results, which is a bad infinity, and to sum an infinite regress is a contradiction. Hegel's idea of the true infinity corresponds to the dialectic of consciousness that functions in the *Phenomenology* itself. The true is the whole because the whole of consciousness is present from the start, and each stage of consciousness is an attempt to make the whole specific. Each such attempt leads to another and to another, each determined within the totality of the whole in a procedure analogous to the functional principle of $\varphi(x)$. True infinity is a process of self-development, such as that inherent in the *Phenomenology* itself.

CHAPTER 9

On Reading the Second "Half" of the *Phenomenology*: An Overview of Reason and Spirit

The *Phenomenology* is divided into three parts: A. Consciousness, B. Self-consciousness, and C., which has no title independent of its internal divisions. A and B make up a unit in that they mirror the two moments of Hegel's dialectic of consciousness in-itself and consciousness for-itself. They are the first "half" of the work in that they are the two moments of the experience of consciousness writ large, and what follows presupposes a grasp of the movement from consciousness to self-consciousness. In terms of pages, these two divisions are much less than half of the work, being only about one hundred pages. Together with the preface, they are less than one-fourth of the text, but in terms of structure the work divides between them and the untitled "C." To look at the *Phenomenology* in terms of its divisions of contents is to see it only in terms of the understanding and not in terms of the internal movement of the dialectic, which is the real order of its thought. But the familiar way of thinking of the understanding is always our starting point, and Hegel, after all, has given the work this overall formal order. How are we to approach its divisions as a guide to keeping in mind its contents and purpose?

The work as published has two general systems of order: a set of capital letters and a progression of eight chapters with Roman numerals. Three of the eight chapters are the contents of A. Consciousness. The fourth is the content of B. Self-consciousness. Thus, in terms of the number of chapters, half of the work is contained in Consciousness and Self-consciousness. The remaining four chapters correspond, respectively, to the remaining divisions: Reason, Spirit, Religion, and Absolute

Knowing. Except for Absolute Knowing, which has no internal subdivisions, there are three large subdivisions within each of Reason, Spirit, and Religion. The movement within each of these subdivisions is from a consciousness toward a self-consciousness of their subject matter. Jon Stewart, in an essay, "The Architectonic of Hegel's *Phenomenology of Spirit*," has pointed out that while both of these systems of order are Hegel's in his drafting of the *Phenomenology*, their combination is likely due to its editors. The copy of the first edition of the *Phenomenology* I have examined in the Vatican Library bears both of these overlapping systems of contents. Despite this artificiality it is possible to understand how the two systems go together. We as contemporary readers are stuck with it.

Major Divisions of the Contents

A. Consciousness
- I. Sense-Certainty
- II. Perception
- III. Force and the Understanding

B. Self-consciousness
- IV. The Truth of Self-Certainty

C. (AA.) Reason
- V. The Certainty and Truth of Reason

(BB.) Spirit
- VI. Spirit

(CC.) Religion
- VII. Religion

(DD.) Absolute Knowing
- VIII. Absolute Knowing

Reason moves from "observing reason," or the application of reason to inorganic and organic processes, to forms of the activity of the ego, to the action of the ego in relation to other egos. In modern terms, this would generally correspond to a movement from the subject matters of the natural to those of the behavioral and social sciences. Spirit moves from various senses of ethical or moral order, given objectively in human nature and divine law, to social morality based on rational justifications, to reflective doctrines of morality and moral conduct. Religion moves from a religion of nature, to a religion of art or made objects, to the personal theism of revealed religion.

These are rough characterizations, but they may help to keep in mind the direction of Hegel's account in each of these divisions, as his own specific titles may seem disconnected and unique. Throughout this second "half" of the *Phenomenology* Hegel seems just to keep writing, moving from one title or subtitle to the next. The reader is best advised just to keep reading what Hegel writes, to move along with Hegel, even if at times it is not apparent where the thought is going, and to keep the general drift in mind. Otherwise, one may become lost in Hegel's cave and not able to catch the ray of light that points the way out.

What I am calling the second "half" of the *Phenomenology*, as I have said, is the untitled Section C. The double (AA.) for Reason suggests that reason is a return to consciousness as a new in-itself. It is the world originally looked at in terms of pure sensation, perception, and understanding, seen from the perspective of the self—the forms of consciousness experienced in a self-conscious way as products of thinking or reason. The double (BB.) for Spirit suggests that spirit is a return to self-consciousness as a for-itself. The dynamics of selfhood of the stage of self-consciousness are what underlie the moral, ethical, and social forms of spirit. Spirit is an expansion and ordering of the primordial struggles among selves portrayed in the stage of Self-consciousness. There is no clear one-to-one correspondence of the stages of A to (AA.) or of B to (BB.), but there seems to be this general re-patterning. We could say that in Hegel's memory theatre of the *Phenomenology* the doubling requires the recollection of the stage that it doubles.

If some sense can be made of the doubling of A and B to produce the stages of Reason and Spirit, what is intended by the doubling of C for (CC.) Religion? Hegel's *Phenomenology* foreshadows the divisions of the *Encyclopaedia of Philosophical Sciences in Outline*. Reason has some correspondence to the *Philosophy of Nature* and spirit to the *Philosophy of*

Spirit. Consciousness and Self-consciousness, as the terms of the total movement of consciousness presupposed by the later divisions, have a place similar to the *Logic* in the *Encyclopaedia.* In saying this I do not mean that the *Phenomenology* is a crude form of the *Encyclopaedia*, or that it can be dissolved into the *Encyclopaedia.* But Hegel's whole system is here from the start. Recall that the *Encyclopaedia*, as an outline, is a work of the understanding, looking back upon what *Vernunft* has established.

The *Encyclopaedia* has *Philosophy of Spirit* as its third part, and *Philosophy of Spirit* ends with its triad of art, religion, and philosophy. The movement from religion to absolute knowing in the *Phenomenology* corresponds to this, in a broad way. Religion is a stage that mixes religion and art, which are kept distinct in the *Encyclopaedia*'s triad. Absolute knowing is correspondent to philosophy in this triad, although presented in a much more lively way in the *Phenomenology.* It would be difficult to convince anyone of the vitality and attractiveness of philosophy as absolute knowing if all we had from Hegel were his pages in the end of the *Encyclopaedia.* I count them among the dullest he ever wrote.

If in "C" of the *Phenomenology* the movement is from nature to spirit, then religion is the doubling of C, because religion is the totalization of nature and spirit. It attempts as a phenomenon to be an *Aufhebung* of the "and" and to unify the natural and the spiritual, but it does this only by means of *Vorstellung*, not by the *Begriff* of *Vernunft.* Thus it is not truly absolute knowing, and, in fact, it is a grand illusion of it. Once "C" is doubled there seems nothing left that consciousness could experience, and it is in danger of being lost in the final misfortune of thought, ending up, we might say, in church instead of in the *agora* of history and the whole world.

What, then, of Hegel's label of (DD.) for Absolute Knowing? There is no single D that is doubled as are the divisions A, B, and C. He could have called this D, making it a fourth division and thus taking it completely outside this second "half" of the work. By labeling it as (DD.) Hegel keeps the status of Absolute Knowing ambiguous; that is, he puts it above C and its doubling (CC.) in Religion, yet by doubling the D of absolute knowing he attaches it to his system of doubling. It is "D" and double "D" at once, completely unique. Absolute knowing knows from a standpoint completely different than any other stage, yet it holds before it the doubleness of the A of consciousness, the B of self-consciousness, and the doubleness of C that has been made out of them, first by Reason and Spirit and then by Religion.

How are we to understand the two systems of organization, the eight chapters and the A, B, C, and their doubles, and DD? The eight chapters give the contents as a progression of stages and, in fact, merge with the divisions of C (Reason, Spirit, and Religion) and DD (Absolute Knowing), in effect repeating the same word of each division. The alphabetical order is static, a juxtaposition onto the progression of chapters. The alphabetical order is a kind of architectonic, yet it is more than that, for it shows how the work recapitulates itself, passing back and forth over itself.

In the end, how seriously should we take the table of contents? Probably no more and no less seriously than we should take the list of contents of any book, especially since not only Hegel but his editor had a hand in forming it. The contents is an outline of the book and for the informed reader it is a clue to how to follow the work. Anyone who has written a work requiring a table of contents knows that the author constructs it carefully. Hegel is no exception, even if he separately created the two orders in drafting the work. The table of contents is not the work itself, but we must be able to interpret it in order to fix in our mind the ordinary sense of the work that can guide its reading.

I suggest that, at least on its initial reading, the second "half" of the *Phenomenology* be read on two levels at once. On the first level the pages must be turned and Hegel's words read. But, unlike with the first "half" of the work, it is not profitable to attempt to master every turn of the dialectic. The divisions of Consciousness and Self-consciousness can be approached in a precise way. They are compact and they must be completely grasped in order to comprehend the rest. As mentioned above, from Reason forward the reader is dealing with large sections of text, and it is easy to become lost, not knowing, at many points, what is being said. The question must be kept in mind as to where Hegel is going in the section, what is happening to the experience of consciousness in it. Without this sense of overview, which requires continual reference to the table of contents, nothing is being gained.

On the second level of reading, the reader should focus on some section or image that organizes a part of that dialectic, or is a key to the whole of it more than its other images or parts. This can be mastered as a *topos* from which to bring forth the essence of Hegel's thought and to recall it after going farther or finishing the work. The whole of the second "half" must be read carefully, but the reader can select points that can be used to hold together the whole of this large work. Once done in this manner, these *topoi* allow the reader both to go farther and to go back and reread.

As explained in my preface, the remarks that follow in this chapter are not intended to be on the same level of detail and interpretation as are those above on consciousness and self-consciousness. Once the two major movements on which the whole work depends are mastered, the second half of the work can simply be read, keeping in mind the general remarks on Reason and Spirit that follow in this chapter and on Religion and Absolute Knowing that follow in the next.

Overview of Reason and Spirit

(AA.) Reason

The certainty of self-consciousness has been torn asunder by its ultimate self-division in the unhappy consciousness. Self-consciousness now turns not just to an apprehension of its own reality but to that which is distinctive to its own reality—reason. *Man is a rational animal.* Should self-consciousness revert to the distinction-making activity of the understanding, it would face the problem of world-inversion. In the unhappy consciousness it has produced an analogue of the inverted world in which the thing-in-itself has become a permanent beyond of being, a "bad infinity." Reason is the key to self-knowledge and the self must reapprehend the object as a work of reason, which is the distinctive medium of the self's own existence.

Reason here is not the speculative reason that Hegel identifies with philosophy. It is "observing reason" (*beobachtende Vernunft*). This is reason that observes or examines the object. It does not "see into" the object in a speculative sense, but it does aim at observing the object from both an inner and outer perspective. It seeks to grasp the object as a whole, not simply in terms of a set of distinctions reflectively derived from the standpoint of the knower. Nature is examined first as inorganic process and then as organic form. The organic involves teleology, in which the inner of the object—its parts—are organized to produce its outer form—itself as a whole—such that, as Hegel says, "*the outer is the expression of the inner*" (par. 262).

In possession of the organic or biological thought, self-consciousness proceeds to apply reason to its own being as an organism having a distinct behavior pattern or psychology. It arrives at logical and psychological laws that are the results of its observation. This done, self-consciousness attempts to take this process one step farther, to observe the mind as it exists in the body. The results are the sciences of physiognomy and phrenology (more correctly, craniology, *Schädellehre*, lit. "skull-doctrine"). Here the attempt to extend the purely observational powers of reason to the mind itself results in equating the mind with a bone. In the one violent passage in the *Phenomenology*, Hegel says: "The retort here would, strictly speaking, have to go the length of beating in the skull of anyone making such a judgment, in order to demonstrate in a manner just as palpable as his wisdom, that for a man, a bone is nothing *in itself*, much less *his* true reality" (par. 339). Hegel concludes his critique of phrenology by saying that the joining of *Geist* or the mind with the skull is no more than what "Nature naively expresses when it combines the organ of its highest fulfillment, the organ of generation, with the organ of urination [*Pissen*]" (par. 346), making an implied wordplay on *Pissen* and *Wissen*.

Hegel's treatment of phrenology is the section of the *Phenomenology* most ignored by Hegel commentators. This is in part because phrenology is today a wholly discredited science, although in Hegel's day it attracted a number of leading figures. I have given this section a full discussion in my *Hegel's Recollection*, as has Alasdair MacIntyre in an essay, "Hegel on Faces and Skulls." Hegel attacks this false science of mind in detail because it is an imitation of the true science of mind. Phrenology should not be mistaken for phenomenology. The difference lies in two key words: *Schädellehre* and *Schädelstätte* (the German term for Calvary or Golgotha, the place of the skull). Hegel, through his quotation of Schiller's poem at the conclusion of his work, associates the absolute knowing of phenomenology with *Schädelstätte*. One doctrine of the skull should not be mistaken for the other. The phrenologists of Hegel's day are the psychological behaviorists of today, who equate consciousness with observable and testable physiological actions, thus claiming an empirical science of the mind. Hegel's science of the experience of consciousness in effect answers the phrenologist or behaviorist with the same position Socrates takes in the *Phaedo* when he, in effect, raises the question: "Do you think these bones and sinews are Socrates?" (98C–99B).

From the degenerate illusion of attempting to observe itself as an external static object, self-consciousness turns to a grasp of itself through the forms of activity distinctive to the individual human being. This results in three types of inward states or motivations that confront their opposites. The first is that of the *homme moyen sensuel*, "the man on the make," "the man out for a good time," as Findlay characterizes it in his *Hegel*. The pursuit of pleasure comes up against the object as an "empty and alien necessity, a *dead* actuality" (par. 363). The second is the *homme de coeur*, "the man of the heart." The heartfelt approach to the world can accept the world only on its own special, subjective terms. Thus, as Hegel says, "the heart-throb for the welfare of humanity therefore passes into the ravings of an insane self-conceit" (par. 377). The third is the *homme de bien*, "the knight of virtue," the man engaged in the pursuit of good, upright modes of action. The knight of virtue wages a fight with the way of the world but it is, as Hegel says, "strictly speaking, a sham-fight which he *cannot* take seriously—because he knows that his true strength lies in the fact that the good exists absolutely in its own right, i.e. brings itself to fulfillment—a sham-fight which he also *dare* not allow to become serious" (par. 386). For the knight of virtue the fight is the thing, and he can simply change causes at will. He is a professional protester.

Self-consciousness, having failed to master the object by pleasure, the heart, or crusading, now makes a final attempt at self-realization by becoming productive. The "spiritual animal kingdom" is a scene of full activity of selves, each busy with its own individual "matters-in-hand." It is the world of the professor-researcher, the businessman, the entrepreneur, the "doer" transforming the object in terms of some limited purpose. It is a world full of humbug (*Betrug*), with each individual feigning to be interested only in the matter-in-hand as an objective project, while trying above all to make it his own. Hegel says: "A consciousness that opens up a subject-matter soon learns that others hurry along like flies to freshly poured-out milk, and want to busy themselves with it; and they learn about that individual that he, too, is concerned with the subject-matter, not as an *object*, but as his *own* affair" (par. 418). In this modern world everyone is busy all the time.

Findlay translates the full title of this section as "The Spiritual Zoo and Humbug, or the Matter-in-Hand [*Das geistige Tierreich und der Betrug oder die Sache selbst*]." *Tierreich* is a general biological term, in the sense of the animal kingdom as opposed to the plant kingdom. It differs from *Tiergarten*, which is properly the term for the institution of a public or private zoo or zoological garden. A possible meaning to associate with *Tierreich* is *ménagerie*, which captures the sense of a sideshow—animals arranged in a tent for the local gawkers and patrons of a traveling circus. A *ménagerie*, in German, is literally a *Tierschau*, an animal show. *Ménagerie* captures the tawdry sense of spiritual forms that hold themselves on display on Hegel's stage, as they are not quite as dignified as the animals arranged in a sedate zoological garden, or the scientific typology of the animal kingdom. This is a stage of humbug, of smoke and mirrors masquerading as genuine or profound forms of the human spirit. The reader senses the speech of charlatans and barkers, pitchmen of the intellect, acting as if they are real thinkers and representatives of true ideas.

It is traditionally thought that what Hegel had in mind as the primary embodiment of this stage was the world of professors and professional scholarship—each scholar and researcher extolling the extraordinary value of his or her own work and eagerly and deeply explaining it to colleagues, who feign interest only to be able to bend the ear of the speaker and other colleagues concerning their own discoveries and distinctions. This is a high portrait of *Betrügerei*, or "humbuggery"—each professor with his or her own self-important world in a total monarchy of forms of thought or mind on display—each animal strutting its stuff for the visitors (those who, either by will or by happenstance, become audience—students, colleagues, the general public). Philosophies distinguish between true and false philosophizing. This section shows Hegel's account of false philosophy.

Hegel's spiritual zoo is a portrait of a meeting of the American Philosophical Association, or any other academic society, in full swing—job-seekers, tenure-track candidates, job-holders, senior professors—all prowling the halls of a large hotel, passing in and out of meeting rooms, reading papers to large or small numbers of partially interested listeners. All of the residents of the zoo, except the job-seekers, are relatively secure in their respective portable cages, each fully occupied with the matter-in-hand—the next business to be done, the next project, article, or book, the next paper to be presented, the next meeting to attend.

Hegel's zoo reminds me of a story told me by Hans-Georg Gadamer. As he told it (and I have since heard slightly variant versions of it): "God wished to create the most beautiful thing in the world, and he created the Professor. The Devil, wishing not to be outdone, decided to create its greatest opposite, and he created the Colleague!" As Hegel's stage shows, the professor and the colleague share in the medium of *Betrug*. Each engages in deceit, the false interest in the projects of the other, in order to pitch his or her own works, to promote his or her own form of humbug. All professional academics are forever busy, unless they are just loafers—the other possibility traditionally offered members of the academy (but progressively becoming limited, because of the administrator's daily need to keep all engaged in some matter-in-hand).

This engagement of the philosopher-academic is of a piece with the engagement demanded by modern technological society at large. The modern academic is a full participant in the world of the media and method. No one has been quicker than the academic to adjust his or her thinking and use of language to the demands of the computer. The educational process, the process of research, of writing, and of thinking itself, occurs now only in terms of the possibilities of the computer and electronic systems. The spark that is to flash forth between the teacher and the student is, increasingly, electronic. As Jacques Ellul says in *The Technological System*, "Using a computer is not enough to make us modern," by which he means: "To consider *one* computer is to stay on the mental level of the gawker at the county fair who goes to see the basket case or the bearded lady. The computer is not a gadget to do things better and faster. Computers are the correlation factor in the technological systems" (p. 101). Academics and the society at large accept the computer as the basis of all human activity. As Ellul rightly notes, "The computer ensemble plays the part of a nervous system in the technological order; all other comparisons are uninteresting, they are childish outbursts or half-baked knowledge" (p. 102).

If, as Hegel's principle holds, "Philosophies are their own time apprehended in thought," we find the forms of this apprehension in the many cages of the spiritual zoo: positivism, historicism, structuralism, logical empiricism, analytic philosophy of language, existentialism, descriptive phenomenology, hermeneutics, cognitive science, narratology, deconstructionism, postmodernism, applied ethics, and so forth. There are almost too many cages to visit before seeing the show in the big top—technological life itself. Both are spectacles, each with its total occupation with the matter-in-hand, whatever at the moment it might be. The spiritual zoo or *ménagerie* is a world of business-as-usual, whether it be the intellectual matters-in-hand of a philosophical movement or the next achievement in technological order-making.

In the activity of the "spiritual animal kingdom," despite its faults, self-consciousness gains confidence that it can make the object into an extension of its own reality through deliberate activity. The result is reason used to make and test laws. Hegel says: "This 'matter-in-hand' is therefore the *ethical* [*sittliche*] *substance*; and consciousness of it is the *ethical* [*sittliches*] consciousness" (par. 420). But what is produced are not truly laws with validity in and of themselves; what is produced are merely commandments. Because these are merely commandments they are open to criticism, and finally "Reason as the giver of laws is reduced to a reason which merely *critically examines* them" (par. 428). The ability of reason to make laws that establish the order of human society reflects back onto the prior interest of reason in its role of discovering laws of nature and psychological laws.

(BB.) Spirit

Reason developed from observation to production, but production only as a manifestation of individuality, a high form of "mineness." The attempt to establish laws simply through reason does not produce society but it does indicate that law is the basis of human society and that law is based in the phenomenon of moral order. Self-consciousness is unable to attain self-knowledge by the direct exercise of its distinct power of reason. *Man is a social animal.* Self-consciousness gives itself over to this further aspect of itself—spirit or *Geist*. *Geist* as a stage in Hegel's *Phänomenologie des Geistes* has a more restricted sense than *Geist* does as the term in Hegel's title. *Geist* as a stage of *Geist* is the appearance of self-consciousness as a fully social or ethical form of being. *Geist* or spirit as the subject matter of phenomenology is the human self in all of its actual guises, including its proto-social, religious, and philosophical forms.

The first stage of spirit is *true* spirit, which is present in the world of *Sittlichkeit* or customary morality. Law originally has the form of custom and is developed through a relationship between divine and human law. The basis of law and society is the family; it governs the relationships between the sexes. This is "true spirit" in the sense that it is what spirit immediately takes itself to be. Spirit is the immediate ethical order that all individuals follow in terms of their customs. This universal rule of custom does not allow for the determinateness of the individual. It dissolves into the phenomenon of "legal status" (*der Rechtzustand*). Hegel says, "This lifeless spirit is an equality, in which all count the same, i.e. as *persons*" (par. 477). Hegel here recapitulates his conception of person as it emerges in the master-servant dialectic, in which to become a *person* is to withdraw from the life-and-death struggle for selfhood and remain as no one in particular. He says here "to describe an individual as a 'person' is an expression of contempt" (par. 480). Person as it reemerges with spirit is a form of moral existence, but it is a form of spirit alienated from itself. Persons exist in a world of persons.

This self-alienated form of spirit can develop; it can be cultivated. Spirit can make itself into something. In the second major section of spirit Hegel employs the term *Bildung*, which combines the idea of human education with the idea of human culture or cultivation. The individual self-consciousness, having the status of a person with equal rights under the law, can develop a career within society through the cultivation of the power of language and the power of wealth. The self, in its attempts to overcome its alienation, becomes vain and witty. Religion emerges at this stage simply as faith, for religion is unable to achieve here a status in and for itself. Religion exists only as the individual's faith. "Pure insight," which is open to each individual, substitutes for profound or systematic thought. Hegel says: "This pure insight is thus the spirit that calls to *every* consciousness: *be for yourselves* what you all are *in yourselves—reasonable*" (par. 537).

The phenomenon of pure insight develops into the phenomenon of enlightenment. Hegel says: "Pure insight only manifests its own peculiar activity in so far as it opposes itself to faith" (par. 540). The opposition of faith and pure insight becomes the struggle of enlightenment with superstition. Enlightenment pushes faith to the point where it loses all of its imaginative content and it is reduced to "a *sheer yearning*." Hegel says at this point: "Faith has, in fact, become the same as Enlightenment, viz. the consciousness of the relation of what is in itself finite to an absolute without predicates, an absolute unknown and unknowable; but there is this difference, the latter is *satisfied* Enlightenment, but faith is *unsatisfied* Enlightenment" (par. 573). Enlightenment, having defeated faith with its dedication to pure rationality, divides itself in two, one part holding that there is an absolute being, which exists beyond actual consciousness and the other part holding that this being is matter. Hegel seems to have in mind the difference between a rationalist first principle and materialist first principle.

Common to both of these approaches is the abstraction of pure self-thinking. They unite in taking utility (*Nützlichkeit*) as their object. Once utility becomes the object it also becomes a goal. This goal ushers in a new stage of consciousness—absolute freedom. Hegel says: "Spirit thus comes before us as *absolute freedom*" (par. 584), and "this undivided substance of absolute freedom ascends the throne of the world without any power being able to resist it" (par. 585). Once rational insight becomes utility anything is possible, anything can be done in its name. In social terms this rationality can justify suspicion, and Hegel says: "*Being suspected*, therefore, takes the place, or has the significance and effect, of *being guilty*" (par. 591). Utility is rational madness. Hegel concludes this section by saying: "Just as the realm of the real world passes over into the realm of faith and insight, so does absolute freedom leave its self-destroying reality and pass over into another land of self-conscious spirit where, in this unreal world, freedom has the value of truth" (par. 595).

In his analysis appended to Miller's translation of the *Phenomenology*, Findlay suggests that Kantian ethics is the outcome of the phenomenon of absolute freedom and terror. Findlay says: "Absolute freedom has as its positive outcome a purely formal moral will, universal as much as individual. The Kantian categorical imperative is the other side of revolutionary destruction" (comment on par. 595, p. 568). In its attempt to actualize itself objectively in the world as *Bildung*, spirit or culture finally arrives at a version of its reality as universal will. This is an Enlightenment ideal that parallels reason as universal. Kant is an Enlightenment thinker. Hegel's account shows that Kant did not arrive at the categorical imperative that is founded on the universal will simply as a matter of philosophical reasoning, as it might appear. Hegel's account offers a new approach, from culture itself, to comprehending the genesis of this sense of universality. The conditions for the categorical imperative are rooted directly in culture and specifically in the self-alienation of spirit as it carries this alienation to the limit of absolute freedom.

How are we to understand this story of the genesis of the Kantian will and its a priori principle of morality? It is a highly original story that remains unknown in Kantian scholarship—that, as Findlay says, the Kantian imperative is the other side of revolutionary destruction. Absolute freedom is not the freedom of the absolute. Freedom for Hegel is always self-determination. The absolute is an individual, which means that it is a concrete universal; in fact, it is the only true concrete universal in which all determinations are *aufgehoben*. The freedom of the absolute, thus, depends upon determinate negation. What is negated in the process of *Aufhebung* is meaningful; that is, the negative is part of the true. All truths are partial. What is true is to be comprehended in terms of what it is at any given moment and what it is not at that same moment. The individual is both what it is and what it is not at once. The dialectic of these two moments, the doubling up intrinsic to the being of the individual as subject, is its life as spirit.

In contrast to the individual are both the particular and the universal. Particulars are in themselves meaningless because they cannot be a true object of thought. As Hegel makes clear, in "Sense-certainty" particulars can be eaten, digested, and so forth, but they cannot be thought. They are not individuals, for individuals bring with them their own meaning as products of the internal process of spirit. Universals are without meaning in themselves because they are void of determination. Hegel makes this clear in the beginning of the *Science of Logic* in which he equates being and nothing. Being and nothing are equivalent because they are equally indeterminate—the universals of universals. As categories of thought they offer the starting points of intellectual determination, and are thus positive.

Absolute freedom is the phenomenon that spirit experiences when it actually attempts to assume the universal as the reality of the self and society. Absolute freedom is the will taken beyond the limits of all social structure. The will as universal has no way to be determinate and is thus pure power. It has no internal principle of self-regulation. Thus it is meaningless in itself. To have any effective form of itself at all, it yields to the phenomenon of the *faction*. The faction is what is able to seize actual power and act in any way it can to make itself the lord and master of all else. Its sense of negation is simply that of the null class. Thus death is meaningless. Death is just pure negation—the loss of life in an attempt by the faction to purify the particular in relation to the universal will.

Absolute freedom is the ultimate sense of freedom, defined as freedom from restraint, as opposed to Hegel's conception of freedom as self-restraint, that is, self-determination. Absolute freedom necessarily engages in a reign of terror in order to purify all that would be a restraint, a limitation, on the purity of the will. The will is rationality in action separate from grounding in any tradition. When absolute freedom finally has nothing positive left in it, the spirit remembers the sense of itself as individual and transfers the sense of the universal will onto the individual as a ground, resulting in Kantian morality. If this should not happen, as Hegel says: "Spirit would be thrown back to its starting-point, to the ethical and real world of culture, which would have been merely refreshed and rejuvenated by the fear of the lord and master which has again entered men's hearts. Spirit would have to traverse anew and continually repeat this cycle of necessity if the result were only the complete interpenetrating of self-consciousness and substance" (par. 594).

The Kantian imperative is as such a positive outcome, but it has dangerous origins. It can slip back quickly to the drive of the faction toward purification. The Kantian imperative still depends upon the phenomenon of absolute freedom, not the freedom of the absolute. The difference is that it is an intellectual, not a social conception of absolute freedom. The moral self remains outside any traditions when it enacts the imperative, and its purpose is to act such that its actions can become a universal law. The emptiness of the stage of absolute freedom is transferred to the Kantian sphere of the critically motivated individual, not the self-determinate individual. Kant's ethical agent is pure in its attempt to acquire its duties through the universal alone, and this leads to the strange and inhuman conclusion that follows from Bernard Williams's criticism of Kant's morality, that when I visit a sick friend I must say I come to visit you out of duty, not out of sympathy! The Kantian position is inhuman, and in his genesis of it from the absolute freedom and terror, Hegel has shown what the basis of its inhumaneness is. In Kantian ethics the self struggles with the lordship and mastery of the empty universal. As Kant says in beginning the *Groundwork of the Metaphysics of Morals*: "It is impossible to conceive anything at all in the world, or even out of it, which can be taken as good without qualification, except a *good will*." It is the sense of "without qualification" that worries Hegel.

Absolute freedom, having shown its destructive power, needs to justify itself. It needs to attempt once again to become certain of itself. It does so by assuming the seemingly benign form of a rational morality (*Moralität*). Utility is given up for a moral view of the world that seeks principles forged through practical reason. As Hegel says, however, we thus "pass over into another land of self-conscious spirit where, in this unreal world, freedom has the value of truth." In this moral *Weltanschauung*, "Self-consciousness knows duty to be the absolute essence [*Wesen*]" (par. 599). Duty replaces utility.

What follows is a further criticism of Kantian ethics, such ethics being based on the distinction between a realm of nature and a realm of freedom. Self-consciousness is moral consciousness that posits duties as its pure form, but there is "nothing sacred about them for the moral consciousness" (par. 605). "Thus," Hegel says, "it is postulated that it is *another* consciousness which makes them sacred, or which knows and wills them as duties" (par. 606). This is Kant's conception of "religion within the limits of reason alone," in which God exists as rational judge. Consciousness can never achieve the pure acts of willing required by the categorical imperative, and is therefore always unworthy in relation to itself and the perfect judge. Hegel says, of moral consciousness: "In regard to its *willing*, it knows itself as a consciousness whose purposes are affected with sensuousness. On account of its unworthiness, therefore, it cannot look on happiness as necessary, but as something contingent, and can expect it only as a gift of grace" (par. 608).

This moral worldview is really a world of duplicity and pretense. On the one hand, consciousness produces consciously its object, and on the other, it acts as though that which it posits has truly objective being. Hegel says: "The moral worldview is, therefore, in fact nothing other than the elaboration of this fundamental contradiction in its various aspects. It is, to employ here a Kantian expression where it is most appropriate, a 'whole nest' [*ein ganzes Nest*] of thoughtless contradictions" (par. 617). Hegel's reference is to Kant's claim in the *First Critique* that the cosmological proof is "*ein ganzes Nest von dialektischen Anmassungen* [a whole nest of dialectical presumptions]." Hegel makes this into a nest of "thoughtless contradictions [*gedankenloser Widersprüche*]." Hegel says that such moral consciousness "is not, strictly speaking, in earnest with *moral* action" (par. 621). The morality of a good will needs to go nowhere, and in fact ends in hypocrisy, never coming to terms with the actual situation of moral life. We are left, Hegel says, with "The antinomy of the moral view of the world, viz. that there is a moral consciousness, and that there is none, or that the validation of duty lies beyond consciousness, and conversely, takes place *in* it" (par. 632).

To overcome this antinomy consciousness attempts to base morality on conscience. Hegel says: "This self of conscience, spirit that is directly aware of itself as absolute truth and being, is the *third* self" (par. 633). He contrasts this to the self of the legal person and the self that has recovered from absolute freedom and formed moral self-consciousness through the will. Conscience at first seems to offer a way to act in the world. "Conscience," Hegel says, "is the moral genius which knows the inner voice of what it immediately knows to be a divine voice" (par. 655). But conscience withdraws consciousness into its own inner being and lacks the power to externalize itself and make itself into a thing. It becomes a beautiful soul (*schöne Seele*), which "lives in dread of besmirching the splendour of its inner being by action and an existence; and, in order to preserve the purity of its heart, it flees from contact with the actual world" (par. 658).

The beautiful soul is the low point in spirit's attempt to have man exist as a social animal. A specific moral outlook has developed in spirit to this point, but in the beautiful soul the social animal withdraws into itself. The beautiful soul was a human type, widely known in eighteenth-century Germany, associated with the religious revival of Pietism. The beautiful soul is morally and intellectually dangerous. It is a degenerate version of the relation of self-consciousness to the absolute, that threatens philosophy itself.

The beautiful soul's illusion about the absolute is an obstacle more grave to the achievement of speculative thought than is unhappy consciousness. At this earlier stage of attempting to reach the absolute as infinite, unchangeable consciousness can become unhappy. But the beautiful soul is happy, self-satisfied. It appears to be the most profoundly poetic, religious, and philosophical of all possible positions. It seems deeply human. Instead it is anti-communal, and its drive for purity and authenticity is the basis for fanaticism and the destruction of love. Never having understood community, the beautiful soul presents an ideal of pure selfhood, a kind of saintly stoicism of self-indulgence—while appearing to stand above both the morality of ordinary life and the difficult task of realizing virtue and moral character.

Undertaken in order to overcome the deadness and abstraction of the self of duty, the self of conscience retreats within itself when threatened and becomes unable to act. Spirit is dissolved back into the inner life of the individual. But conscience claims to be not just the voice of the self but the voice of the divine, and the stage is set for religion, in which the divine is manifested in a communal activity that can present morality in concrete images.

CHAPTER 10

Absolute Knowing

On each stage of the *Phenomenology*, consciousness has the illusion that it has discovered the absolute, that it has found the way to unify the two moments of itself and make itself whole. But as each stage elaborates itself it discovers that it is only another signpost on the highway of despair. Consciousness pushes on, with each new beginning seeming to be the answer to its self-separation. Hegel's principle, that we learn only one thing from history: that we learn nothing from history, applies also to this process of consciousness. In fact, this constant self-forgetting of consciousness is the root of this truth about history. The stage of Religion is no exception to this repetition of illusion. As consciousness develops, each stage involves a grander sense of illusion because each stage is more complicated and more determinate in its content.

Religion is almost absolute knowing, but it is not absolute knowing. Most commentators emphasize that religion is the absolute realized as the object of consciousness, but that religion's form of knowledge is not that of the *Begriff*. This approach implies that in the succeeding stage of absolute knowing the content of religion is *aufgehoben*. It is true that religion is taken up into absolute knowing. To see the relationship of religion and absolute knowing in this way is to forget that the process of *aufheben* involves not only the raising up of a previous stage of consciousness into a succeeding stage, but that this process is also one of cancellation. Religion is not one side of a coin and absolute knowing the other. Religion does not differ from absolute knowing or philosophy in degree. It differs in kind, as does every other stage of consciousness as it is succeeded by another. Philosophy is close to religion in their common interest in the ultimate ground of experience, but until philosophy separates from religion it has no chance at self-identity. How does religion differ in kind from philosophy or absolute knowing?

In "Revealed Religion," spirit encounters itself in relation to the divine. Within the shape of itself as religion, spirit moves from encountering itself in the externality of the divine forms of nature to the divine as the result of its own production; that is, religion in the form of art. In revealed religion, spirit turns to the divine as the essence of its own internal being as self, but it can never fully reach its own being in this manner. This is because spirit as revealed religion cannot truly *think*. Its thoughts occur as *Vorstellungen*—as something placed before spirit or mind but not truly of it. As revealed religion, spirit has its truth *presented* to itself, but its truth does not appear to revealed religion as something that it has *made* out of itself. Thus revealed religion is not truly self-knowledge. Self-knowledge requires a way for the self to return to itself. This return must be the grasping by the self of itself, not the *presentation* of itself to itself. What keeps religion from being absolute is this element of presenting the truth, even though what is presented is internalized.

Religion is the last grand illusion. It is the illusion that *vorstellen* is the synthesis or unity of the two moments of consciousness—in-itself and for-itself. *Vorstellung* or presentational-thinking seems the perfect mediated-immediacy. Unlike the pure poetical image, the scriptural image carries an intellectual or conceptual meaning as part of its essence. It appears as concrete thinking, and it is, but this is bought at the price of self-knowledge. This self is known to itself through the presentation, just as the reality of the self is ultimately to be found in God. The presentation is external. To inwardize it requires constant effort. This is why scripture is constantly being interpreted. The meaning of the image of the Lord is constantly being spoken about. This occurs in various forms, from sermons to scriptural hermeneutics.

There is an echo here of the "bad infinity" of the unhappy consciousness. The absolute cannot be something placed before the mind; it must be actually realized as spirit knowing itself. How can this be accomplished? Spirit must give up its last grand illusion—that its certainty and truth can be *vorgestellt*. Religion is an extended prelude to absolute knowing. In religion we find the first true glimpse of the absolute. It is a sense of the absolute that is thought and felt at once, in the sense that scripture is based on the power of the image also to yield an intellectual meaning. Thought in the sense of *vorstellen* is scriptural thinking. Such thinking is reasonable but it is not truly speculative.

Hegel's chapter on "Absolute Knowing" falls into two parts. The first is a recollection of the path spirit has followed to reach the point of absolute knowing (pars. 788–98). The second begins with his declaration of what absolute knowing is: "It is spirit that knows itself in the shape of spirit, or a *comprehensive knowing* [*begreifende wissen*]" (par. 798), and continues to the end of the chapter. In this second part, Hegel strikes up two themes: that spirit as absolute knowing is self-knowledge, and that the key to this self-knowledge is recollection (*Erinnerung*). Self-knowledge requires spirit to release itself freely into itself, something it is unable to do fully as religion. Hegel says: "This release of itself from the form of its self is the supreme freedom and assurance of its self-knowledge [*dieses Entlassen seiner aus der Form seines selbsts is die höchste Freiheit und Sicherheit seines Wissens vom sich*]" (par. 806).

Hegel uses the term *Erinnerung* four times in the final paragraph of the work, to explain finally the nature of the *Phenomenology*. In his second mention of *Erinnerung* in this paragraph, Hegel hyphenates it as *Er-Innerung* (par. 808). The hyphenation of the word emphasizes the sense that the process of recollection is "an inwardizing" (*Innerung*). But it further makes the word itself internally dialectical. The substantive, *Erinnerung*, has as its corresponding verb *erinnern*; *er* when compounded with a verb is inseparable, and generally indicates (1) the beginning of the action; it can also indicate (2) the achievement of the aim set by the action. So to speak, *er* in itself is a circle capable of indicating beginning as well as end. *Er-*, as hyphenated, is a pun on *Ur-*, which as a prefix to a noun, indicates origin, source, very old, or primitive. *Erinnerung* has within it a dialectical circle that moves from origin to its inwardizing, from being in-itself to being for-itself. The hyphen stands for the "and" between the two that is ever-present as a separation yet a necessary connection in their being. Hegel's use of wordplay that makes philosophy speak German begins with his pun on *Meinung* at the opening of the *Phenomenology*, and continues to its closing lines, with his hyphenation of *Er-Innerung* as the master key to his science.

The two-part format of the chapter on absolute knowing reflects Hegel's two-part division of the introduction, in which he first recapitulates the state of current understanding of truth related to the fear of error, and then, in the second half, he displays in general the method of truth. In Absolute Knowing he summarizes the general path consciousness has taken in the shapes of the phenomenology and then states the nature of absolute knowing. Like the introduction, it says what its subject is not and then says what it is.

As Hegel summarizes the movement of consciousness up to absolute knowing, he says it begins with the thing as the object of immediate knowing, progresses to the thing as the object of observing reason, in which the "*being of the 'I' is a thing*" (par. 790), to the "I" as the self of spirit. From spirit emerge both religion and the total shapes of spirit itself, which Hegel says exist as two sides. From the side of religion, Hegel says, consciousness is reconciled with self-consciousness in the form of *being-in-itself*. From his vantage point, spirit appears to be the resolution of consciousness and self-consciousness in terms of *being-for-self*. He says: "The unification [*die Vereinigung*—uniting, combining, bringing together] of the two sides has not yet been exhibited; it is this that closes the series of the shapes of spirit, for in it spirit attains to a knowledge of itself only as it is *in itself* or as possessing an absolute *content*, nor only as it is *for itself* as a form devoid of content, or as the aspect of self-consciousness, but as it is both *in essence and in actuality*, or *in and for itself*" (par. 794).

Absolute knowing is the "bringing together" of the two sides of the self. These two sides are parallel to the ancient definition of wisdom that Cicero preserves—that wisdom is a knowledge of things divine and human (*Tusc.* IV.26.57). Religion is the self in the shape of the divine. Spirit, with its form of ethical life and culture, is the self in the shape of the human. Wisdom, or what Hegel calls absolute knowing, is the joint apprehension of the two. It is the concentration on the "and" that brings together the two sides. Wisdom is a meditation on the "andness" of the world. "And" is inherently dialectical, and wisdom is the acceptance that the nature of experience is dialectical. To be wise is to know this. This is what absolute knowing, knows. It is absolute because it is different from all other forms of consciousness in both degree and kind.

As absolute, this knowing has no illusions of the synthesis or simple unity of the two forms of being, the two sides. The divine and the human remain separate but conjoined. This must be accepted. Prior to attaining the stage of absolute knowing, the self is unable to accept this fact of the "and." It pursues, in shape after shape of itself, the illusions of the unification of these two forms of being—the being of the object and the being of itself or the object for itself. Its highway of despair does not yield divine knowledge, but it yields peace—the freedom to release itself as dialectical consciousness, as ironic consciousness, in the sense that the meaning of "andness" can only be pointed to and never literally stated.

Hegel reminds the reader that substance becomes subject and that "Spirit necessarily appears in time" (par. 801). He also very clearly says that "the movement is the circle that returns into itself, the circle that presupposes its beginning and reaches it only at the end" (par. 802). The form of the life of selfhood is time. Its being is in time. But time, for Hegel, is dialectical; it is not historical in its essence. The transformation of substance into the self as subject is temporal. Temporality is a movement through opposites. Time is a time "projected," a project of spirit. Time is not simply a set of historical conditions that bound the self. The project of spirit is to find within itself the moment of absolute knowing. This project is a circle because it requires the self to come back upon itself, to return to its own beginning.

Return of the self to itself is recollection. To recollect, as Aristotle says in *On Memory*, is to put what is remembered into an order. The order into which the self puts itself is a dialectical movement. This is speculative because it requires a "seeing into." Recollection is the self seeing into itself as subject, not as object nor as the "I" as object. Time, as dialectical order, appears in the form of the self's recollection, and does not exist for the self as a preestablished order. The progression of the shapes of the self is not contingent but necessary. Since the self that recollects is actual, it could not be otherwise. The self's project in recollecting its being is to comprehend the sense in which it could not be otherwise. It is thus engaged in recollection, not just in the formation of memories.

Absolute knowing as self-knowing in the above sense has no content in itself. Its content is only its own recollections of the shapes of the highway of despair. Phenomenology is recollection. It is a memorial method, not a descriptive method, as Husserl would have it. Husserl's phenomenology, for all its value, is a literal-minded, still-standing philosophy. Without dialectic Husserl can offer no speculative or recollective knowledge. Thus autobiographical knowledge is excluded from the start. The Hegelian phenomenology is in the end the autobiography of consciousness. It is the solution of the ancient problem of wisdom and self-knowledge through the introduction of "autobiographical knowledge." Hegel's phenomenology is, then, the graphic life of the self—the *autos bios graphē*. In the phenomenology of Hegel, the human self appears in speech, in language. The self is made through the word; the word is the power distinctive to human existence. To make the knowledge of the self through the word, then, is to engage in the act that is the key to the human and to the world of spirit.

Hegel brings descriptive phenomenology together with speculative phenomenology. Each stage of consciousness in Hegel's "science of the experience of consciousness," if taken by itself, is an exercise in descriptive phenomenology, at least in principle. Hegel attempts to give an accurate and direct description of a specific stance of consciousness. But the *Phenomenology* is not simply a collection of all these various stances. Coupled with Hegel's descriptive method is a genetic method. Consciousness not only fixes itself in particular stances, it develops itself by passing from one stance to another, as an individual develops from childhood to maturity. Consciousness is not simply to be conscious in a certain way but to be in self-motion. Consciousness, as is implied in the German word *Bewußtsein*, is a being (*Sein*) toward knowing (*wissen*).

Knowing as an act of self-motion or self-development is essentially autobiographical. The *Phenomenology* is the story of the human self writ large, a story that finds its beginning at the point where the phenomenon of doubt enters consciousness and certainty becomes a problem that is first only felt and then later thought. The *Phenomenology* is a work written for those who have in some way already encountered wonder, that Aristotle says is the beginning of the love of wisdom. In the *Phenomenology* the reader finds something of what is already there in the reader's prior experience. Slowly the descriptions of each stage make sense and the genesis of one in the other is familiar. Hegel's highway of despair has recognizable signposts that allow the reader to descend into the reader's own memory to find the commonplaces the individual shares with consciousness in general. Ultimately the validity of Hegel's philosophy, like the validity of any philosophy, rests on the ability of his readers to remake Hegel's story as their own.

Has Hegel's making of human self-knowledge failed or succeeded? In the preface he says he will turn the ancient love of wisdom into actual wisdom. Has he done this? He has, in that he has produced a new conception of recollection that comes to grips with time in a way different from Platonic recollection of the forms. But he has not annulled time completely. He says this in his modification of Friedrich Schiller's poem on "Friendship" (*Die Freundschaft*) at the end of the *Phenomenology*: "from the chalice of this realm of spirits / foams out to Him His infinity" (my trans.). The lines express the Godhead as witness to His own forms of spirit. But in this act of witnessing or conscience, the divine is not brought together with the forms witnessed. They are only conjoined as friends are conjoined, yet other. It is the final, melancholic picture in the "Gallery of Pictures," the *Gallerie von Bildern*. But it is the picture of wisdom. Wisdom or absolute knowing is the final realization by consciousness that the double *Ansich* forever remains double. Its two moments, no matter in what particular form, what particular content they occur, are divided by an absolute gap, a beyond that is not outside consciousness but within consciousness itself, and that is the abiding condition of its experience. Hegel's absolute is the standpoint from which consciousness can again go forth back into the world—but this time it suffers from no illusion.

Consciousness knows without question that every dialectical structure collapses into another. This wisdom is a practical wisdom, or prudence, a guide to acting in the world, of confronting every situation with a foreknowledge of the principles of its dialectic, the way in which the oppositions within any situation will affect each other. What else is wisdom than an absolute standpoint that allows the self to know itself in any situation and move with success within the human world, free from the illusions that hold ordinary consciousness in their grasp?

In Hegel's absolute, philosophy advances from a love of wisdom to an actual wisdom of human affairs, a prudence of life and thought established through traveling the whole course of the highway of despair. In the end, absolute knowing is a knowing only the philosopher knows. It is what the philosopher requires to be in the world, to attain the philosophic life based on the mastery of opposites. The double sense of all things is what the Hegelian philosopher brings to the world. This double sense of things is what is attained by the ascent to the absolute.

APPENDIX

Hegel's Terminology

1. Das Absolute (the Absolute)

Hegel uses "absolute" as a noun throughout his text. Note that it functions as an adjective in the titles of the three conclusive moments of his system: *Das absolute Wissen*, "Absolute Knowing" (in the *Phenomenology*); *Die absolute Idee*, "The Absolute Idea" (in the *Science of Logic*); and *Der absolute Geist*, "Absolute Spirit" (in the *Encyclopaedia*). *Das Absolute* (from *absolut*, adj.) is as close as Hegel comes to having a truly technical term. Note Findlay's remark in the foreword to the Miller translation on Hegel's note for republication of the *Phenomenology* in 1831—that an abstract Absolute dominated when the work was originally written (see Johannes Hoffmeister's appendix in the Meiner edition, p. 578).

2. An sich (in itself), für sich (for itself), das Ansich, das Fürsich, das Ansichsein, das Fürsichsein, das Anundfürsichsein (being-in-and-for-itself)

Hegel uses the terms *an sich* (in-itself) and *für sich* (for-itself) in several combinations. His discussion of these terms is concentrated in his introduction, but they occur throughout the text. Another concentration of these terms is in the final chapter on "Absolute Knowing." He makes *an sich* into a noun, *das Ansich* (the in-itself) (see, e.g., pars. 85–86), and *für sich* into *das Fürsich* (the for-itself) (see, e.g., par. 802). He also connects them with being (*Sein*), thus: *das Ansichsein* (being-in-itself) and *das Fürsichsein* (being-for-itself). He makes both into the compound *das Anundfürsichsein* (being-in-and-for-itself) (see, e.g., par. 24). *An sich* and *für sich* are the two poles of Hegel's conception of the dialectical self-movement of consciousness. Through its presence in consciousness the object that initially has being-in-itself comes to have being-for-itself. It becomes something for consciousness.

In this connection Hegel also employs the term *für uns* (for us) (see, e.g., par. 83). *Für uns* is associated with Hegel's conception of the *wir* (the "we") to which he refers from time to time. It is problematic as to who the *wir* is at any given point in Hegel's exposition, but in general the *für uns* refers to we who are attempting to know the truth of the object, to make it not something simply in-itself but something "for us." This is parallel to the process consciousness undergoes in its own self-movement of transforming the object as an in-itself into an object for it—the movement of what is in-itself to what is for-itself. Note that when Hegel puts the terms *an und für sich sein* together as *Anundfürsichsein* the conjunction *und* remains. They are never combined by Hegel as "*Anfürsichsein*" ("being-in-for-itself"). The *und* always stands between the *an* and *für*. They are always conceived as a conjunction.

Hegel also uses terms related to this complex such as *das Andere* (the other), *Ansichselbstsein* (being-in-itself), *für ein anderes* (for an other), *Füreinanderessein* (being-for-another), *Sein für anderes* (being for another), *an und für sich selbst* (in-and for-itself), *für es* (for it).

Insichsein = "inwardness," a term Hegel uses in connection with the "beautiful soul" (see par. 795).

3. Aufhebung, aufheben, aufgehoben

Aufheben is a verb used in ordinary German that has no genuine equivalent in English. It has been rendered as "supersede" and by a combination of two English verbs, such as "cancel" and "preserve" (as well as by "transcend," "sublate"). *Aufheben* is the noun that describes such action; *aufgehoben* is the past tense of *aufheben*. Hegel also uses *das Aufgehobene*, what has been *aufgehoben*. *Aufheben* is Hegel's term for the way in which one stage of consciousness is transformed into a succeeding stage, the sense in which a preceding stage is replaced yet absorbed into and incorporated in a new way into a succeeding stage. A basic metaphor for this is the way in which within any human being the world of the child is transformed into the world of the adult and the relationship between any of the stages and substages along the way.

Aufheben is not a mysterious or technical term and is used in ordinary German conversation. It has four basic English meanings and Hegel is exploiting all of them at once to convey his dialectical sense of development. *Aufheben* can mean: (1) to lift or raise something up, as in the simple sense of the verb *heben*, "to raise"; (2) to take something up, to pick it up or even seize it actively (a seeming intensification of the act of *heben*, "*auf*"-*heben*); (3) to keep or preserve something, to retain it; and (4) to abolish, annul, cancel, to put an end to something. Depending on the context, *aufheben* can be used in ordinary speech to emphasize one or more of these senses. Often readers of Hegel have made too much of this term. The basic concept of development that Hegel is drawing on certainly exists for the English-speaking mind, but the concept cannot be expressed in a single transitive verb. *Aufhebung* or *aufheben* designates a theory Hegel has of the developmental and dialectical nature of consciousness.

Hegel defines what he means by *Aufhebung* in his discussion of "Perception," par. 133.

4. BEGIERDE (DESIRE)

Hegel's term associated with the rise of self-consciousness. See esp. "Masterhood and Servitude," pars. 190ff.

5. BEGRIFF (CONCEPT), BEGREIFEN, GREIFEN

Begriff is translated by both Baillie and Miller as "notion." Walter Kaufmann, in his translation of Hegel's preface in *Hegel: Texts and Commentary*, and Kenley Dove, in his translation of Hegel's introduction printed in Martin Heidegger's *Hegel's Concept of Experience*, translate *Begriff* as Concept (capitalizing the first letter). "Notion" (Latin: *notio*) and its counterparts in French, Italian, and Spanish is from *noscere*, *notum*, to know. Its first meaning in the *O.E.D.* is: "a general concept under which a particular thing or person is comprehended or classed;

a term expressive of such a concept." Findlay has argued for notion as the proper English translation. But notion in ordinary speech is often used to designate the indefinite, accidental mental apprehension of something as opposed to the actual, knowledgeable grasp of something. "Having a notion" of something in ordinary discourse often connotes having a kind of figurative grasp of something that is close to what Hegel means by *Vorstellung* (a nonconceptual representation). *Vorstellung* for Hegel is the opposite of the *Begriff*. Hegel's *Begriff* is a "concrete universal" in which the particular is formed in a dialectical, nonabstractive manner and by means of which consciousness can think or know a thing as it actually is. In ordinary German, *Begriff* = concept.

The best solution may be to render *Begriff* simply as "concept" (with a lowercase "c") and let its special meaning emerge in the text, just as Hegel does in the original with the ordinary term *Begriff*. Consider the connection of *Begriff* with the verb *begreifen* (to understand, comprehend, conceive, grasp) and its connection with *greifen* (to seize or grasp in a physical sense, as with the hand). Also, *der Griff, die Griffe*—grip, grasp, handle, handles.

6. Das Bewußtsein (consciousness)

Note that the German word is made of *bewußt* (adj.), known, aware, and *Sein*, being. To be conscious is to exist or be in a state of knowing or awareness. English: "conscious" (Latin: *conscius*, from *con* + *scire*). Consciousness is a root term for Hegel, which he frequently falls back on to explain other terms, although they ultimately also explain what consciousness is. *Selbstbewußtsein* = self-consciousness.

7. Das natürliche Bewußtsein (natural consciousness)

Natural consciousness is consciousness that is only potentially knowledge, that has not undertaken the development of the *Begriff* within itself (par. 78). Hegel says that when natural consciousness attempts to enter into science, it must learn to "walk on its head" (par. 26).

8. Das unglückliche Bewußtsein (the "unhappy" consciousness)

Hegel's term for the final stage of B. Self-consciousness. The translation of *unglücklich* by "unhappy" is not an entirely happy one. The German term is connected to *Glück* (happiness, luck) and *Unglück* (misfortune, woe, accident). The "unhappy consciousness" is not simply a state of unhappiness, which might change by being cheered up. In this stage consciousness feels hapless, ill-fated. *Unglück*, although the negative of *Glück*, is a much stronger idea than "unhappy."

9. Bildung (formation, education, culture)

Die Bildung is a key word in the title of the second section of Hegel's presentation of *Geist* in the *Phenomenology*. Here it has the specific meaning of culture or civilization as a world of values that exists as an "other" to the individual. Ethical spirit first located in the abstract individual agent is transposed to the social world that now forms an ethical other to the individual ethical spirit. Both Baillie and Miller translate *Bildung* here as "culture."

Bildung is a term for which there is no clear-cut English equivalent; it can be variously translated depending upon the context. Hegel uses the word variously throughout his text. The verb *bilden* means to form, fashion, shape, model, and it can mean in its reflexive form (*sich bilden*) to form, arise, develop. *Bilden* can also mean to educate, train, discipline, cultivate, improve, and *sich bilden* to improve one's mind. Someone who is *gebildet* is educated, cultivated, cultured. Hegel's *Phenomenology* as a whole has been described as a *Bildungsroman*—as being like that form of the novel that relates in narrative the self-development, education, rising to cultural maturity of a central character, the central character in Hegel's work being consciousness itself.

Bildung in ordinary German can mean, among other things: formation, shape, structure, development, growth, generation, education, training, cultivation, culture, civilization. It might be likened to the Greek word *paideia* (see the first page of Werner Jaeger's *Paideia*, vol. 1, for a description of all its meanings). *Bildung* often has the sense of the "spiritual formation" (and thus presupposes the unique meaning of the German sense of *Geist*) of consciousness or a consciousness. In this sense it combines the ideas of education and culture; it refers to the level of cultivation of spirit, which is different from formal education. In this sense it is like what is classically meant in English by an "educated person," someone whose being is of a certain sort, who has cultivated in his own consciousness what his culture has preserved and developed. But *Bildung* can refer to the process itself, not just to it as it exists in individual experience.

10. Dasein

One of the terms of ordinary German made famous by Heidegger and now frequently left untranslated in philosophical literature. Hegel uses it throughout the *Phenomenology*, giving it his own philosophical meanings but attaching no special meaning to it such as it has in Heidegger's *Being and Time*. One of the meanings given in standard German dictionaries is *das Vorhandensein*, and *Existenz* is given as a synonym. *Das Vorhandensein* = existence, presence. The verb *vorhanden* (something that plays a role in Heidegger's philosophy) has the sense of what is on hand, present, in stock, extant. The normal translation for *Dasein* is "existence." It is literally "being-there" (*da* = there, *Sein* = being). It also can have the sense of *Leben* (life) as in "a beggar's life," "a beggar's existence." *Dasein* is what is there, and the being of which consists in just being there: existence, what is present.

11. Dialektik

Dialektik is much discussed in relation to Hegel's philosophy but not much discussed as a term by Hegel. Hegel uses the term, for example, *die dialektische Bewegung* (dialectical movement), referring to the manner in which consciousness develops in relation to its object. Hegel speaks more of the "self-movement of the concept [*Begriff*]," which is dialectical in form. Hegel associates this dialectical movement with the form of speculative thought, especially the "speculative sentence or proposition" (see Preface, par. 61ff). He calls Plato's *Parmenides* the "greatest artistic achievement of the ancient dialectic" (par. 71). Hegel's dialectic is unlike dialectic as it is commonly understood. It is not the simple posing of opposites, or the generation of probabilities. It is not connected to argumentation. Hegel's dialectic is also not a method in the ordinary sense of an instrument that can be applied externally to a subject matter. Dialectic refers to the actual and necessary form of consciousness as it develops in relation to its object and to the form that speculative knowing takes when it makes this development explicit.

Hegel never describes his own dialectic as having the form: *thesis-antithesis-synthesis*. In the preface (par. 50) he associates this sense of "triplicity" with a type of philosophical Formalism deriving from Kant, which he strongly rejects. Most commentators do not use this threefold scheme to describe Hegel's dialectic; W. T. Stace is an exception. Karl Rosenkranz, Hegel's friend and author of the first serious book on Hegel's philosophy, does not use this description. But it is a characterization that has persisted, probably because it makes a difficult philosophy simple to grasp.

12. Einsicht (insight)

This is a term Hegel opposes to "edification" (see par. 7). He also opposes the term "scientific insight" (which he associates with true thought and the work of the *Begriff*) to the mentality of "common sense" (see par. 70). These senses of *Einsicht* are different from Hegel's use of it to characterize the stage of *Geist* entitled "Faith and Pure Insight," a sense of insight Hegel criticizes.

13. Entfremdung, Entäußerung (estrangement, alienation)

Hegel entitles the second section of *Geist* "Der sich entfremdete Geist" ("Self-estranged Spirit"). *Entfremdung* is literally estrangement (*fremd* = foreign, strange). At the beginning of this section Hegel relates *Entfremdung* to *Entäußerung* (see par.

485), which is "alienation." Miller, however, translates *Entäußerung* here literally as "externalization." The reflexive verb *entäußern* has the sense of parting with, depriving someone of something, divesting someone of something. Marxist readers of Hegel focus a great deal on this section (as well as that of the master-servant), where the self is alienated from collective consciousness. Hyppolite, in his commentary, makes a great deal of Hegel's use of *Entäußerung* (see *Genesis and Structure*, pt. 5, sec. 3). It should be noted that although Marxist thought makes a great deal out of the concept of alienation, *Entäußerung* is not a widely used term in Hegel's *Phenomenology*.

14. ENTSPRECHEN, SICH ENTSPRECHEN (CORRESPOND TO, MEET)

This is the verb Hegel frequently uses regarding the relationship of concept and object. *Entsprechen* = answering, suiting, matching, being in accord with, meeting with, corresponding. NB that it conveys only a notion of correspondence or accord; there is no sense of making identical with or unifying with.

15. ENTZWEIUNG (DIREMPTION, SUNDERING)

Baillie translates this by the obsolete "diremption," which is quite suggestive, meaning forcible separation; Miller uses "sundering." *Entzwei* (adj.) = "in two." See Hegel's account of the inverted world, par. 162. Miller also uses "diremption," but not necessarily as a translation of *Entzweiung* (see, for example, par. 136).

16. ERBAUUNG (EDIFICATION)

Hegel's term for the mentality that wishes to synthesize philosophically all things into the identity of the whole. Such thought produces a feeling of the whole but does not allow us to think the whole through the differentiations of the *Begriff*.

17. ERFAHRUNG (EXPERIENCE)

Hegel calls the *Phenomenology* the "Wissenschaft der Erfahrung des Bewußtseins" ("Science of the Experience of

Consciousness"). *Erfahren* = come to know, experience; *fahren* = to travel. To have experience, consciousness must move between opposites.

18. Erinnerung (recollection)

Miller sometimes translates this as "memory" (see, for example, par. 13), but the word in German for memory is properly *Gedächtnis*. *Erinnerung*, like recollection, is not simple remembering or mental retention but the power to recall what is already in consciousness and make it known again. "Recollection" does not contain in its construction as a word the sense of "inner" that is obvious in the German, *Erinnerung*. On the final page of the *Phenomenology*, Hegel uses *Erinnerung* four times in four different ways to summarize the standpoint of the *Phenomenology*, at one point hyphenating it as *Er-Innerung* to bring out the sense of the inner (*inner*, adj.; *das Innere*). Recollection is a way consciousness acts toward itself within itself, and in this "innerness" it is analogous to the dialectical self-movement wherein consciousness brings forth a knowledge of its own being. From time to time Hegel uses the verbs *erinnern* and *sich erinnern* (reflexive) and at crucial points speaks of consciousness "forgetting" itself and the path of development it has traveled.

19. Erkennen (cognition, knowledge)

Erkennen (the noun from the verb *erkennen*) is the term Hegel uses as the title for his preface—"Vom wissenschaftlichen Erkennen." This may be best rendered, as it is by Miller, as "On Scientific Cognition." *Wissen* and *Erkennen* in a sense both mean "knowledge" or (as verbs) "to know." But *Wissen* is the term that Hegel associates with the sense of knowing of his own philosophy, as in the title of his final chapter—"Das absolute *Wissen*." Terms that define *erkennen* in standard German dictionaries are *wahrnehmen*, *sehen*, *unterscheiden* (perceive, see, distinguish or discern). *Erkennen* has the sense of knowing in the sense of recognizing or being aware of something, apprehending something. "Cognition" is an appropriate

English term because it refers to the process of knowing or the act or capacity of knowing. *Wissen* is more properly "to know" and is part of *Wissenschaft*, a term that Hegel appropriates for his system as a whole. In the preface Hegel concentrates on describing various kinds of thinking or knowing and contrasting them to his own kind of true scientific knowing. This may be why Hegel uses *Erkennen* in the preface, both in its title and frequently in its text. There are various kinds of "scientific cognition" but only one true form of "scientific knowing."

Anerkennen (recognition) is the term associated with the struggle of one individual consciousness to be recognized by another in Hegel's master-servant relationship.

20. Erscheinung (appearance)

Note its connection with *Schein* ("apparency"), the term originally used by Johann Heinrich Lambert in his conception of a phenomenology or science of appearance. (See Hoffmeister's introduction to the *Phänomenologie des Geistes*.)

21. "Galerie von Bildern" (Gallery of Images or Pictures)

What Hegel calls the *Phenomenology* at the end of the work (see par. 808). *Bild* = picture, image.

22. Gegenstand (object)

The Latinate *das Objekt* exists in German. *Gegenstand* is the ordinary German word for object—something that can be perceived or thought in some fashion. *Gegenstand* is Hegel's common term for what consciousness knows or confronts as its direct other. Taken apart, *Gegenstand* is: *gegen* (prep.), meaning over against, contrary to, opposed to; and *Stand*, standing or upright position. *Gegenstand* = "what-stands-over-and-against."

23. Geist (spirit)

Unlike the first term of his title, *Phänomenologie*, Hegel uses the second term of his title, *Geist* (*des Geistes* = the genitive form), throughout his work. Baillie translates *Geist* as "Mind" and Miller translates it as "Spirit." "Mind" is too limiting a term for the German term *Geist*, especially in Hegel's context, because of the way mind has come to be understood in classical British epistemology and Anglo-American psychology. *Geist* has many meanings in German, as spirit does in English, including the idea of "ghost" and "holy spirit," and can, as in English, refer to "alcoholic spirits." Standard German dictionaries give the first meaning of *Geist* as *Atem* or *Hauch*—"breath"—breath as the bearer of life. Following this it gives: "das denkende, erkennende Bewußtsein des Menschen" ("the thinking, cognizing consciousness of humans"); *Art, Beschaffenheit, Wollen, Streben, Gesamtheit aller nichtmateriellen Eigenschaften* ("manner, nature, will, aspiration, totality of all nonmaterial qualities") as applied to the spirit of a people, the spirit of an age; *Mensch im Hinblick auf seine vestige Fähigkeiten, sein inneres Wesen* ("human being in regard to his spiritual abilities, his inner being"). Spirit in contemporary English is not an equivalent of *Geist.*

Geist is a powerful and flexible word in German intellectual literature, especially among thinkers in the nineteenth century. A. L. Kroeber and Clyde Kluckhohn's study of the term "culture" shows that in Hegel's time *Geist* replaces *Cultur*. They point out that in the late 1700s J. C. Adelung uses the phrase "Cultur des Geistes"; Kant in his *Anthropologie* speaks about *Cultur* and in the *First Critique* describes metaphysics as the completion of the culture of reason; Fichte discusses *Cultur* and *Vernunftcultur*. But *Cultur* in this period is largely understood in its original eighteenth-century sense as "cultivation." Hegel always uses *Geist* (see Kroeber and Kluckhohn, *Culture*, pp. 35–44).

Geist for Hegel expresses the interconnection between the mental, spiritual, and willful properties of the human individual and the collective activities that make up human culture—art, religion, theoretical thought, and so forth. And it also includes what in French is called *moeurs* (as, for example, in Rousseau's *Discourses*)—"manners, habits, customs, ways, morals." These realities—individual, social, cultural—which exist as *Geist* "show" themselves as phenomena. They are "appearances" that can be described in language and conceptually formed as parts of a total process, developmentally and dialectically comprehended.

24. GESETZT (POSITED)

Hegel uses this a great deal in the *Science of Logic* but also in the *Phenomenology*. The term *gesetzt* (p.p. and adj.) means fixed, set, placed, established; *setzen* is the ordinary verb in German for to place, set, put. *Gesetzt* is traditionally translated as "posited," which has a very "philosophical" sound and preserves nothing of the very ordinary sense of *setzen*.

25. GEWIßHEIT (CERTAINTY)

As in *Die sinnliche Gewißheit*, "sense-certainty," *Die Wahrheit der Gewißheit seiner selbst*, "the truth of self-certainty," and *Gewißheit und Wahrheit der Vernunft*, "the certainty and truth of reason." Note that the theme of "certainty" runs through Hegel's first three major divisions of the *Phenomenology*—A. Consciousness, B. Self-consciousness, and C. Reason.

26. GLEICH (LIKE)

Gleich = the same, like, equal, equivalent, alike, similar, resembling, proportionate. This is a term Hegel uses to describe the relationship between appearance and essence (*Wesen*). NB that *gleich* cannot mean "identical" (*identisch*).

27. HERRSCHAFT UND KNECHTSCHAFT (MASTERHOOD AND SERVITUDE)

Both Baillie and Miller translate this "Lordship and Bondage," which is more of an interpretation than a translation, since these English terms connote the feudal period of European society of lords of the manor and serfs attached to them in bondage. These terms need not necessarily have these meanings. *Herrschaft* is from *Herr* (master, the modern "Mister," Mr.), *Knecht* = lit. servant. Sometimes this is incorrectly called

Hegel's stage of "master-slave." *Der Knecht* is not slave, which is literally *der Sklave. Der Knecht* can be used for slave only in a figurative sense.

28. Lust (pleasure)

Hegel's term for the section "*Die Lust und Notwendigkeit*" ("Pleasure and Necessity"). *Lust* does not ordinarily have the meaning of sexual desire but the generalized meanings of pleasure, delight, inclination, desire, wish (as in *Wanderlust*). Carnal lust is more closely *sinnliche Begierde* (sensual desire). This section is, however, Hegel's portrait of the "man of pleasure"—the "man on the make," as Findlay has called it.

29. meinen, das Meinen (to opine, opinion, "Meaning")

Hegel opens the *Phenomenology* with a pun on this word that cannot be duplicated in English because English does not happen to use similar words for the two senses on which Hegel wishes to make his wordplay. The pun is on the first-person possessive pronoun *mein* (mine) and *das Meinen* (opinion). Hegel uses the noun from the verb *meinen* (to mean, to opine). The ordinary noun is *Meinung*, as in *meine Meinung* ("my meaning, "my opinion," "my view"). "Meaning" is an awkward translation of *das Meinen*, but is used by both Baillie and Miller. The common German term for "meaning," in the sense of something having a meaning, is *Bedeutung*.

30. Der gesunder Menschenverstand (common sense)

Ordinary German term for "common sense." Literally: "sound or healthy human understanding." See Hegel's attack on common sense as a substitute for philosophizing (pars. 68–69). Also see his short piece "*Wer denkt abstrakt?*" ("Who Thinks Abstractly?"), translated in Kauffman's *Hegel: Texts and Commentary*.

31. Moment (moment)

As in "a moment of consciousness." Any particular stance or standpoint consciousness assumes in its dialectical development.

How consciousness is fixed on its object at any given point. It can have the sense of aspect; the aspects of something are its different moments.

32. Die bestimmte Negation (determinate negation)

Hegel's concept of negation differs from that used in traditional logic, in that negation for Hegel does not represent a null class. Negation is never "empty" for Hegel. In the self-movement of consciousness, when something is affirmed by consciousness to exist and be an object of knowledge for it, to have a truth for it, something is at the same time denied or negated. What is negated has content; there is something specific that is being negated even though it is not then explicit to consciousness in its act of knowing. But to know the truth of its object fully, consciousness must know it in relation to its opposite—what it has negated in order to affirm the object before it (see par. 78).

33. Die Arbeit des Negativen (labor of the negative)

See Hegel's preface, par. 19. Some of Hegel's other comments on the negative in the preface are in his discussion of death in par. 32: "*die ungeheure Macht des Negativen* [the tremendous power of the negative]," and he speaks of "staring the negative in the face and tarrying with it." Hegel says that of all things death is the most dreadful.

34. Phänomenologie, das Phänomen (phenomenology, phenomenon)

The first use of the term *Phänomenologie* as part of a philosophical system is as a section title in a work by the eighteenth-century thinker Lambert, "*Phänomenologie oder Lehre vom dem Schein* [Phenomenology or Doctrine of Appearance]," the short title of which is *Neues Organon.* Lambert's book appeared in 1764. In 1770 Kant wrote to Lambert of the need for a negative science to precede metaphysics, to be called a general phenomenology (*Phaenomenologia generalis*). In a letter to Marcus Herz, Kant wrote that he intended to write such a phenomenology. The possibility of a "science of phenomena" or "phenomenology" is established in Kant's distinction between phenomenon and noumenon as the terms through which German idealism was founded. (See Hoffmeister's introduction to the *Phänomenologie des Geistes*.)

Hegel does not make any special use of the term *Phänomen* itself, nor does he have any particular discussion of it in his preface or text of the *Phenomenology*. Hegel simply employs *Phänomenologie* as the general term for his "Science of the Experience of Consciousness." But it may be useful to keep the dictionary meaning of the term "phenomenon" in mind. Hegel, as does Kant, takes it from Late Latin *phaenomenon* (from Greek *phainomenon*, neut. pres. part. of *phainesthai*, to appear, passive of *phainein*, to show). A phenomenon in its dictionary sense is any object known through the senses rather than through thought or intuition. From Kant forward it is an object of experience susceptible to philosophical or scientific description. As with Lambert's title above, *Phänomen* is connected in its Greek roots to the German *Schein*, "apparency," that is part of the term which Hegel frequently uses, *Erscheinung*, "appearance."

35. Schädellehre ("Phrenology")

Schädellehre (*Schädel* = skull, *Lehre* = doctrine) is the term Hegel used for the pseudo-science of phrenology. It is literally translated as "craniology" but is given as "phrenology" by both Baillie and Miller. *Schädellehre* is the original term for this "science," used by its founder, Franz Joseph Gall, and it was the only term by which Hegel knew it at the time of writing the *Phenomenology*. *Phrenologie* was coined later.

36. Schädelstätte (Golgotha, Calvary)

Schädelstätte (*Schädel* = skull, *Statte* = place), place of the skull or Golgotha (the mount on which Christ was crucified), is used by Hegel to describe his conception of *Geist* on the final page of the *Phenomenology*.

37. Sein, das Seiendes (Being, a being)

Heidegger's famous terms, but also used by Hegel and the German language generally (although not in Heidegger's particular sense of the "Being of beings"). *Sein* is the standard term for Being. *Ein Seiendes* is something that is, being in the sense of a particular existent thing, being in a particularized sense (for example, see Hegel's use of *ein Seiendes* in "Sense-certainty," par. 96). Ontologically *Seiendes* carries the sense of being as multiple as opposed to Being which is always one. But these are not special terms of Hegel's philosophy, as they are of Heidegger's.

38. Die schöne Seele (the beautiful soul)

Part of the final stage of Hegel's theory of *Geist*. *Die schöne Seele* is taken from the sixth book of Goethe's *Wilhelm Meisters Lehrjahre*. It is a human type widely known in eighteenth-century Germany, connected with the revival of Pietism. As with all of Hegel's stages, however, it is also a universal type of consciousness not tied to a given historical example.

39. Sittlichkeit (customary morality)

This is the first stage of Hegel's theory of *Geist*. *Sittlichkeit* has no exact English equivalent. It is not simply morality. It is specifically the sense of morality determined by custom or social practices within human groups. Hegel contrasts this with *Bildung* and *Moralität*.

40. Das Spekulative, die spekulative Philosophie (speculative philosophy)

Hegel understands his sense of philosophy to be speculative philosophy (See Preface, pars. 56–57). Hegel uses the term "reflection" (*Reflexion*) but "speculative" is what he uses to characterize his form of philosophy. Hence the title of the first philosophical journal founded in America—*The Journal of Speculative Philosophy* (founded by those followers of Hegel known as the St. Louis Hegelians). In Preface, par. 37, Hegel speaks of "*Logic* or speculative philosophy," referring to the work to follow the *Phenomenology*.

41. Der spekulative Satz (the speculative sentence or proposition)

Miller translates *Satz* as "proposition," but it can be translated as "sentence." Translating it as "proposition' reflects the principle in ordinary logic, that different sentences that are rewordings of each other express the same proposition. Hegel discusses the idea of "the speculative sentence" in the preface (see pars. 61ff). He says that the distinction between subject and predicate is destroyed in the speculative sentence. The speculative sentence is based on an inner dialectical movement that moves from subject to predicate and back in the direction of subject, but now in a new sense. The speculative sentence defines what it means to think speculatively and provides Hegel's model of what philosophical language is. It suggests that Hegel's *Phenomenology* is a construction of such philosophical sentences.

42. Subjekt

As Hegel states in the preface, he wishes to show in the *Phenomenology* that Substance (*Substanz*) is essentially *Subjekt* (par. 25).

43. System

Hegel calls the *Phenomenology* the first part of his "system of science." In the *Phenomenology* Hegel refers to his philosophy as a circle (par. 18) and in his *Science of Logic* Hegel says his system is a circle and in fact "a circle of circles."

44. Das geistige Tierreich (the spiritual animal kingdom)

Hegel's term for the stage of individuality formed through reason. *Tierreich* is literally "animal realm or kingdom." Findlay in his *Hegel* translates this quite nicely as "spiritual zoo," although zoo is *Tiergarten*.

45. Der Ritter der Tugend (the "knight of virtue")

Hegel's term for the figure he describes in the section on "Virtue and the Way of the World" (see, for example, par. 386).

46. Unendlichkeit (infinity)

See Hegel's paraphrase of the lines of Schiller's poem "Friendship" at the end of the *Phenomenology*. In the *Science of Logic* Hegel explains his famous distinction between the "bad infinite" (*Schlecht-Unendliche*), the infinity that goes on and on and the "true infinite" (*wahrhaft Unendliche*), his special sense of an infinity in which the whole systematically recapitulates itself. This distinction has relevance to the understanding of the so-called stage of "unhappy consciousness" in the *Phenomenology*. Hegel uses the term *schlechte Unendlichkeit* in his criticism of physiognomy (see par. 322).

47. Verdopplung (doubling)

In his account of the "unhappy consciousness" Hegel speaks of the *Verdopplung*, the "doubling" or self-duplication of consciousness (see par. 206). *Gedoppelte* = doubled.

48. vergessen (to forget)

Vergesslichkeit (forgetfulness) is the counter term to *Erinnerung* (recollection). Hegel speaks of consciousness entering into a new stage by forgetting the path it has traveled to get there and thus discovering what it takes to be a completely new world. This is how, for example, Hegel presents the transition from the stage of "Self-consciousness" to "Reason" (see par. 233).

49. verkehren (turn topsy-turvy, invert), die verkehte Welt (the topsy-turvy or inverted world)

This is tied to Hegel's term "*die verkehrte Welt*" (the "topsy-turvy world" or "inverted world"). Hegel also uses the words *Verkehrung* and *Verkehrtheit*. Hegel's phrase derives from Ludwig Tieck's play, *Die verkehrte Welt* (1799). Grimm's *Deutsches Wöterbuch* cites Sebastian Brant's *Narrenschiff* (*Ship of Fools*, 1494) as a source for the verb *verkehren*. Hegel's discussion of the *verkehrte Welt* comes at the end of A. Consciousness, before the appearance of B. Self-consciousness, but he uses *verkehren* to describe the motion of consciousness at several points in the text. *Umkehren* is the verb for turning back, return, reversal. No English verb quite captures the sense of *verkehren*, which is the notion of inversion in a perverse manner, the notion of turning everything upside down and introducing confusion into a situation.

50. Vermittlung (mediation)

A term associated with the dialectical action of consciousness on its object. *Vermitteln* = to mediate. *Mittel* is "means." *Unmittelbar* (adj.) is "immediate." To mediate something is to gain it or affect it through an intermediate agency or condition, to attain it not directly or "immediately" but through a means or medium that is not directly the thing itself. Consciousness always comes to the object as mediated, as existing in its own medium—in the medium of itself—because even when consciousness apprehends the object in its "immediacy" (*Unmittelbarkeit*), it is actually apprehending something already formed through an earlier stage of consciousness. Thus "immediate" and "mediate" become relative terms within the totality of the self-movement of consciousness. For Hegel's explanation of mediation see par. 21.

51. Vernunft (reason)

Hegel endorses the idea of *Vernunft* against *Verstand* ("the Understanding"). The understanding allows us to classify and order the world but it can give no knowledge of the whole. Only reason can be dialectical in form. The "speculative sentence or proposition" is the thought-form of reason. The understanding cannot get beyond the propositional form of ordinary logic that keeps the subject and predicate separate. Hegel calls the understanding a "table of contents" mentality (see Preface, par. 53). Hegel's sense of the *Begriff* is closed to the formalism of the understanding but is open to and in fact is the life of reason.

52. Verstand (the Understanding)

Miller makes a point of translating this as "the Understanding" to emphasize Hegel's distinction between it and reason. It also functions in Hegel's text in its ordinary sense of "understanding."

53. Der Weg der Verzweiflung (highway of despair)

Hegel's phrase for what natural consciousness undergoes when it undertakes to follow the stages of the phenomenology of spirit and achieve absolute knowing (see par. 78).

54. Vorstellung (picture-thinking, figurative thinking)

This is Hegel's contrasting term to thought done in the true philosophical form of the concept (*Begriff*). Hegel also characterizes the stage of consciousness that he calls "Religion," the stage immediately before that of "Absolute Knowing," as a stage in which thought has the shape of *Vorstellungen* (picture-thoughts). *Vorstellung* is not easily translated by any single English term that will suit all or most contexts. It is a flexible and easily used term in German. The verb *vorstellen* literally means "place before" (*vor* = before; *stellen* = to place). *Vorstellen* is to present, represent, put forward, mean, signify; as a reflexive (*sich vorstellen*) it is to imagine, suppose, conceive. *Das Vorstellen* can be used to mean "the imagination" (but also *Einbildungskraft* = imagination). *Vorstellung* is the term used for a performance, as a theater performance. It can mean: imagination, idea, notion, conception, mental image. In the preface (par. 58) Hegel calls the habit of thinking in terms of *Vorstellungen* a kind of "material thinking," a kind of contingent consciousness absorbed in material stuff. *Die Vorstellung* is placing something before the mind or consciousness as an image, a picture, a presentation, a vague idea. It is to be actually thinking a thought (as opposed to merely having a sensation or perception), but to be thinking the object in less than a true conceptual form (as understood in Hegel's sense).

55. Das Wahre (the true), die Wahrheit (truth)

"*Das Wahre ist das Ganze*" ("The true is the whole"), Preface, par. 20. Note that Hegel uses "the true" in this famous statement, not "the truth." Hegel often speaks of the "truth of" something (*die Wahrheit* of something), as in his titles of chapters 4 and 5: "The Truth of Self-certainty" and the "Certainty and Truth of Reason." In the preface he speaks about types of truth (*Wahrheit*). But "the true" is the word he associates with the whole. *Das Wahre*, as Hegel uses it, has an active sense of something made by consciousness, rather than a "truth" that is found out about something or asserted of something.

56. Wesen (reality, essence, being)

A term used widely in German philosophy that has multiple meanings and can be variously translated according to context. It is a contrasting term to *Dasein*. Standard German dictionaries give the definition of *Wesen* as a philosophical term as: "*Sosein der Dinge, im Unterschied zum blossen dasein*" ("the being thus and so of things as distinct from mere existence"). The *Wesen* of something often has the sense of its inner nature or being—its essence—what it is in reality, apart from the accidental conditions of its existence.

57. Widerspruch (contradiction)

Not a term Hegel makes a great deal out of, but one that some commentators and critics have overused.

58. wir (the "we")

The first-person plural that Hegel uses to refer to the consciousness that is witnessing the phenomenology of consciousness presented in the text. Hegel mentions the "we" at various points. It is both a rhetorical device and a systematic principle of his phenomenology. What Hegel means by the *wir* and whether it has different senses of reference and meaning at different points has been explored very little in standard commentaries. Hegel also uses *für uns*, a term closely associated with the *wir* (see, for example, pars. 25 and 83; cf. par. 122).

59. Wirklichkeit (actuality)

What is real or actual is *wirklich*. This is the term Hegel uses in the famous quotation "the real is the rational," as it is sometimes translated (the comment is made by Hegel in the preface to the *Philosophy of Right*). *Real* (adj.) (real, actual) and *das Reale* (something real) exist in German, as does *Realität* (reality). But *aktuell* is "topical," what is current, the latest: *Aktualität* = topicality. Where English might use "reality," German would use *Wirklichkeit*. *Wirken* = effect, do, bring about, produce.

60. Wissenschaft (science), das Wissen, wissen (knowing, to know)

Wissenschaft is translated by both Baillie and Miller as "science" or "Science." This is a problematic term in English because of its contemporary connection with the natural, social, and behavioral sciences, which are experimental in nature. *Wissenschaft* does not have this limitation of meaning in Hegel's time or in contemporary German. Standard German dictionaries define *Wissenschaft* as: "*geordnetes, folgerichtig aufgebautes, zusammenhängendes Gebiet von Erkenntnissen*" ("an ordered, logically built up, coherent field of knowledge"). *Wissenschaft* = the root meaning of science, namely, knowledge obtained by study, any department of systematized knowledge. Consider Hegel's designation of his work as "Science of the Experience of Consciousness."

Hegel wishes to keep *Wissenschaft* in contact with its root meaning of *wissen* (to know). *Wissen* is to have knowledge of something, to have something in consciousness (*im Bewußtsein haben*). *Das Wissen* is knowledge or knowing, as in the title of the last chapter of the *Phenomenology*—"*Das absolute Wissen*" ("Absolute Knowing"). Hegel's *Wissenschaft*, a term that he identifies with his whole system, is intended not as a particular field of knowledge alongside other fields but as something identified with knowledge and knowing itself.

Works Cited

Aristotle. *Posterior Analytics*; *Topics*; *De Anima; On Memory*; *History of Animals*. In *The Complete Works of Aristotle*, 2 vols., ed. J. Barnes. Princeton, N.J.: Princeton University Press, 1984.

Bacon, Francis. *Sylva sylvarum, or A Natural History in Ten Centuries*. In vol. 2 of *The Works of Francis Bacon*, ed. J. Spedding, R. L. Ellis, and D. D. Heath. New York: Garrett, 1968.

Bayer, Thora Ilin. *Cassirer's Metaphysics of Symbolic Forms: A Philosophical Commentary*. New Haven, Conn.: Yale University Press, 2001.

Bayle, Pierre. *Historical and Critical Dictionary*, selective trans. R. Popkin. Indianapolis, Ind.: Hackett, 1991.

Brandt, Sebastian. *The Ship of Fools*, trans. E. H. Zeydel. New York: Columbia University Press, 1944.

Cassirer, Ernst. *An Essay on Man: An Introduction to a Philosophy of Human Nature*. New Haven, Conn.: Yale University Press, 1944.

———. *The Philosophy of Symbolic Forms*, vol. 2, *Mythical Thought*, trans. R. Manheim. New Haven, Conn.: Yale University Press, 1955.

———. *The Philosophy of Symbolic Forms*, vol. 3, *The Phenomenology of Knowledge*, trans. R. Manheim. New Haven, Conn.: Yale University Press, 1957.

Cicero, Marcus Tullius. *Tusculan Disputations*, trans. J. E. King. Vol. 18 of *Cicero in Twenty-Eight Volumes*. Cambridge, Mass.: Loeb Classical Library, Harvard University Press, 1989.

———. *Academica*, trans. H. Rackham. Vol. 19 of *Cicero in Twenty-Eight Volumes*. Cambridge, Mass.: Loeb Classical Library, Harvard University Press, 1994.

Collingwood, R. G. *An Autobiography*. Oxford: Clarendon, 1939.

Descartes, René. *Discourse on the Method of Rightly Conducting One's Reason and Seeking the Truth in the Sciences*. In vol. 1 of *The Philosophical Writings of Descartes*, trans. J. Cottingham, R. Stoothoff, and D. Murdoch. Cambridge: Cambridge University Press, 1985.

———. *The Correspondence*. Vol. 3 of *The Philosophical Writings of Descartes*, trans. J. Cottingham, R. Stoothoff, D. Murdoch, and A. Kenny. Cambridge: Cambridge University Press, 1991.

Eliade, Mircea. *Cosmos and History: The Myth of the Eternal Return*, trans. W. R. Trask. New York: Harper Torchbooks, 1959.

Ellul, Jacques. *The Technological System*, trans. J. Neugroschel. New York: Continuum, 1980.

Encyclopédie, ed. Denis Diderot and Jean Le Rond d'Alembert. Paris, 1751–80.

Feldman, Burton, and Robert D. Richardson, eds., *The Rise of Modern Mythology 1680–1860*. Bloomington: Indiana University Press, 1972.

Fernald, Daniel Horace. *Spirit's Philosophical* Bildung: *Image and Rhetoric in Hegel's Phenomenology of Spirit and Science of Logic*. Lanham, Md.: University Press of America, 2004.

Findlay, J. N. *Hegel: A Re-Examination*. London: Allen and Unwin, 1958.

Frazer, James George. *The Golden Bough: A Study in Magic and Religion*, abr. ed. New York: Macmillan, 1958.

Gadamer, Hans-Georg. *Truth and Method*, 2nd rev. ed., trans. J. Weinsheimer and D. G. Marshall. New York: Crossroads, 1982.

Goethe, Johann Wolfgang von. *Wilhelm Meisters Lehrjahre*. Vols. 17 and 18 of *Goethes Sämtliche Werke*. Stuttgart and Berlin: J. G. Cotta'sche, 1902.

Hegel, G. W. F. *Philosophy of Right*, trans. T. M. Knox. Oxford: Clarendon, 1942.

———. *The Phenomenology of Mind*, trans. J. B. Baillie, rev. 2nd ed. London: George Allen and Unwin, 1949.

———. *Phänomenologie des Geistes*, ed. J. Hoffmeister. 6th ed. Hamburg: Meiner, 1952.

———. *On Christianity: Early Theological Writings*, trans. T. M. Knox. New York: Harper Torchbooks, 1961. Includes the fragment on "Love" and the "System of 1800."

———. *Hegel's Political Writings*, ed. Z. A. Pelczynski, trans. T. M. Knox. Oxford: Clarendon, 1964.

———. *Science of Logic*, trans. A. V. Miller. London: Allen and Unwin, 1969.

———. *The Encyclopedia of Philosophical Sciences in Outline*: Part I: *The Logic of Hegel*, trans. W. Wallace, rev. A. V. Miller. Oxford: Clarendon, 1975; Part 2: *Hegel's Philosophy of Nature*, trans. A. V. Miller. Oxford: Clarendon, 1970; Part 3: *Hegel's Philosophy of Mind*, trans. W. Wallace, rev. A. V. Miller. Oxford: Clarendon, 1971.

———. *The Difference between Fichte's and Schelling's System of Philosophy*, trans. H. S. Harris and W. Cerf. Albany: State University of New York Press, 1977.

———. *Faith and Knowledge*, trans. W. Cerf and H. S. Harris. Albany: State University of New York Press, 1977.

———. *Phenomenology of Spirit*, trans. A. V. Miller. Oxford: Clarendon, 1977.

———. *Hegel: The Letters*, ed. Clark Butler; trans. Clark Butler and Christiane Seiler. Bloomington: Indiana University Press, 1984.

———. *The Jena System, 1804–5: Logic and Metaphysics*, trans. J. W. Burbidge and G. di Giovanni. Kingston and Montreal: McGill-Queen's University Press, 1986.

Heidegger, Martin. *Being and Time*, trans. J. Macquarrie and E. Robinson. London: SCM Press, 1962.

———. *Hegel's Concept of Experience*, trans. K. R. Dove. New York: Harper and Row, 1970.

Hesiod, *Theogony*. In *Hesiod, Homeric Hymns, Epic Cycle, Homerica*, trans. H. G. Evelyn-White. Cambridge, Mass.: Loeb Classical Library, Harvard University Press, 2002.

Homer. *The Iliad*, trans. Robert Flages. New York: Penguin Books, 1998.

Husserl, Edmund. *Ideas: General Introduction to a Pure Phenomenology*, trans. F. Kersten. Vol. 2 of *Collected Works*. The Hague: Nijhoff, 1982.

Hyppolite, Jean. *Genesis and Structure of Hegel's Phenomenology of Spirit*, trans. S. Cherniak and J. Heckman. Evanston, Ill.: Northwestern University Press, 1974.

Jaeger, Werner. *Paideia: The Ideals of Greek Culture*, 3 vols., trans. G. Highet. New York: Oxford University Press, 1945.

Joyce, James. *Ulysses*. Paris: Shakespeare and Company, 9th printing, 1927.

Jung, C. G., and C. Kerényi. *Essays on a Science of Mythology: The Myth of the Divine Child and the Mysteries of Eleusis*, trans. R. F. C. Hull. Princeton, N.J.: Princeton University Press, 1969.

Kant, Immanuel. *Groundwork of the Metaphysics of Morals*, trans. H. J. Paton. New York: Harper and Row, 1956.

———. *Critique of Pure Reason*, trans. N. Kemp Smith. London: Macmillan, 1958.

———. *Critique of Judgment*, trans. J. H. Bernard. New York: Macmillan, 1974.

Kaufman, Walter, trans. and ed. *Hegel: Texts and Commentary*. Garden City, N.Y.: Doubleday Anchor, 1966.

Kojève, Alexandre. *Introduction to the Reading of Hegel: Lectures on the Phenomenology of Spirit*, trans. J. H. Nichols, Jr. New York: Basic Books, 1969.

Kroeber, A. L., and Clyde Kluckhohn. *Culture: A Critical Review of Concepts and Definitions*. New York: Vintage Books, orig. pub. 1952.

Lévi-Strauss, Claude. *Introduction to the Science of Mythology*, vol. 1, *The Raw and the Cooked*, trans. J. and D. Weightman. New York: Harper Torchbooks, 1969.

Locke, John. *An Essay Concerning Human Understanding*, ed. A. C. Fraser, 2 vols. Oxford: Clarendon, 1989.

MacIntyre, Alasdair. "Hegel on Faces and Skulls." In *Hegel: A Collection of Critical Essays*, ed. Alasdair MacIntyre. Notre Dame, Ind.: Notre Dame University Press, 1976.

Magee, Glenn Alexander. *Hegel and the Hermetic Tradition*. Ithaca, N.Y.: Cornell University Press, 2001.

Manuel, Frank. *The Eighteenth Century Confronts the Gods*. Cambridge, Mass.: Harvard University Press, 1959.

Mueller, Gustav E. "The Hegel Legend of 'Thesis-Antithesis-Synthesis.'" In *The Hegel Myths and Legends*, ed. J. Stewart. Evanston, Ill.: Northwestern University Press, 1996, pp. 301–5. Orig. pub., *Journal of the History of Ideas* 19 (1958): 411–14.

Parry, David. *Hegel's Phenomenology of the "We."* New York: Lang, 1988.

Piaget, Jean. *L'épistémologie génétique*. Paris: Presses Universitaires de France, 1972.

Plato, *Phaedo*; *Theaetetus*; *Parmenides*. In *Plato, Complete Works*, ed. J. M. Cooper. Indianapolis, Ind.: Hackett, 1997.

Quintilian. *The Orator's Education (Institutio oratoria)*, 5 vols., trans. Donald A. Russell. Cambridge, Mass.: Loeb Classical Library, Harvard University Press, 2001.

Rosenkranz, Karl. *Hegels Leben*. Berlin, 1844.

Rousseau, Jean-Jacques. *The First and Second Discourses*, trans. R. D. Masters and J. R. Masters. New York: St. Martin's, 1964.

———. *Essay on the Origin of Languages*, trans. V. Gourevitch. New York: Harper and Row, 1986.

The St. Louis Hegelians, 3 vols., ed. M. H. De Armey and J. A. Good. Bristol, England: Thoemmes Press, 2001. Selections from the *Journal of Speculative Philosophy*.

Schelling, F. W. J. *Philosophie der Mythologie*, 2 vols. Darmstadt: Wissenschaftliche Buchgesellschaft, 1976.

Schiller, Johann Christoph Friedrich von, "Die Freundschaft." In vol. 1 of *Sämtliche Werke*, ed. G. Fricke and H. G. Göpfert, in connection with H. Stubenrach, 6th ed. Munich: Haner, 1974–80.

Smith, John H. *The Spirit and Its Letter: Traces of Rhetoric in Hegel's Philosophy of Bildung*. Ithaca, N.Y.: Cornell University Press, 1988.

Stace, W. T. *The Philosophy of Hegel: A Systematic Exposition*. New York: Dover, 1955; orig. pub. 1924.

Stewart, Jon. "The Architectonic of Hegel's *Phenomenology of Spirit*." *Philosophy and Phenomenological Research* 55 (1995): 747–76.

Tieck, Ludwig. *Die verkehrte Welt*. In vol. 5 of *Ludwig Tiecks Schriften*. Berlin: Georg Reimer, 1828–46.

———. *The Land of Upside Down*, trans. D. Mandel. London: Associated University Presses, 1978.

Tylor, E. B. *Primitive Culture*. London, 1871.

Verene, Donald Phillip. *Hegel's Recollection: A Study of Images in the Phenomenology of Spirit*. Albany: State University of New York Press, 1985.

———. *Philosophy and the Return to Self-Knowledge*. New Haven, Conn.: Yale University Press, 1997.

Vico, Giambattista. *The New Science*, trans. T. G. Bergin and M. H. Fisch. Ithaca, N.Y.: Cornell University Press, 1984.

Whitehead, Alfred North. *Process and Reality: An Essay in Cosmology*. New York: Macmillan, 1929.

Williams, Bernard. *Ethics and the Limits of Philosophy*. Cambridge, Mass: Harvard University Press, 1985.

Index